FLOWER
DECORATIONS

THE SOLITUDE OF MR POWERS

Once there was a lovely man named Mr Powers.
He was lonely because his wife fixed flowers.
Mr Powers was a gallant husband, but whenever he
wished to demonstrate his gallantry
His beloved was always out with six vases and a bunch
of something or other in the pantry.
He got no conversation while they ate
Because she was always nipping dead blossoms off the
centrepiece and piling them on her plate . . .

◆

Finally he said Hey!
I might as well be alone with myself as alone with a lot
of vases that have to be replenished everyday,
And he walked off into the dawn,
And his wife just kept on refilling vases – never
noticed he was gone.
Beware of floral arrangements;
They lead to marital dis-arrangements.

Ogden Nash

FLOWER
DECORATIONS

A NEW APPROACH
TO ARRANGING FLOWERS

Fleur Cowles

with the assistance of
Susan Conder

GALLERY BOOKS
An Imprint of W. H. Smith Publishers Inc.
112 Madison Avenue
New York City 10016

To T.M.M.
Flower Lover

First published in 1985 by
Conran Octopus Limited
37 Shelton Street
London WC2H 9HN

This edition published
by Gallery Books in
1989 in association
with Conran Octopus Limited

Edited by Susan Conder

Art Director: Douglas Wilson

Designed by Bridget Heal

Photographs on pages 1-10, 14-124 by Philip Dowell

ISBN 0-8317-3399-3

Typeset by Hourds Typographica
Printed and bound in Hong Kong

CONTENTS

INTRODUCTION 6

FLORAL POWER 9
The Language of Flowers ◆ Changing Tack ◆ Wild Flowers

TABLE MANNERS AND ROOM SETS 19
High Rise ◆ Low Life ◆ Faces Only ◆ High Drama ◆ Occasional Charm

EDIBLE DELIGHTS 41
Cabbages and Kings ◆ Fruitful Ideas ◆ Leafy Greens ◆ Floral Food

GREEN AND PLEASANT 53
Variegated Foliage ◆ Colour Choice ◆ Generic Delights

CHEATING THE SEASONS 65
Potted Plants and 'Pot-et-Fleur' ◆ Forcing the Issue
Fruitful Thoughts ◆ Fabulous Fakes ◆ Dried and Preserved Flowers ◆ Pressing Matters
Artistry and Aftercare ◆ Pot-Pourri

JARDINIERES AND JAM JARS 93
Pots and Pans ◆ Dressing Up and Seeing Through ◆ Weaves and Woods
Talls and Smalls ◆ Do's and Don'ts

LIFE-LONG TECHNIQUES 105
A Longer Life for Cut Flowers ◆ Buying the Best ◆ First Pick
Conditioning ◆ Aftercare ◆ Cut Flower Nutrient ◆ Special Problems
Second-hand Rose ◆ Tools and Technicalities ◆ Floral Balls

A FLORAL PALETTE 125
Floral Foibles ◆ Floral Favourites

SPECIALLY PROTECTED WILD PLANTS 141

ACKNOWLEDGEMENTS 142

INDEX 143

INTRODUCTION

As a writer and a painter, I've always been addicted to flowers. Flowers, in fact, live on my mind. I need and love them. I'm unhappy without them and, inspired by years of affection, they're stored away in a mental diary.

◆

This book is written for everyday, everywhere flower-lovers who want to enhance their creative and often unawakened skills in using flowers – who love ideas, who appreciate originality but hate eccentricity, who may have only a modest budget.

◆

Today, flowers are more than decoration: they are our calendars, they are messages of love, they bring joy to the sick, happiness to the lonely, they make poets of the unpoetic, artists of amateurs. And they force us all to know a little more, perhaps unwittingly, of botany and ecology.

◆

There is no geography to flowers – they even grow near the poles of the earth – and wherever they do grow, they are treasured. Peasants need to be surrounded by them; conservationists re-seed fields to replace those disappearing; magnates employ botanists and staffs of gardeners. In every level of society, women buy them as automatically as bread, and to some they are just as essential.

◆

If you, too, love flowers (and I don't know anyone who is actually indifferent to them) you, too, would be unhappy without them in your life – frustrated if you didn't find new ways to use them. A home without them is bare, lifeless, cold; with them, you provide a form of your own autobiography since a room is really like a personal museum. Even a kitchen glass holding one lovely rose makes the home more welcome, personalized and friendly.

◆

Although my love affair with flowers has been life-long, and my quest for using them in original, unpretentious and untraditional ways equally long-standing, this book is far from fanatic. Its aim is to stir you, guide you, even lure you into trying out new ideas with flowers, and to bring to flower arranging an attitude free of traditional restraints. No extra time or money is called for, simply an open mind and the will to experiment. I've spent a lifetime not only inventing but accumulating new ideas. My homes in London, Sussex and Spain are always decorated with flowers, and they are as important to me as the furniture and paintings. Each home is different in feel, and the flowers available are different, too, but the approach remains the same.

I am an admitted renegade. Professional rules bore me to tears – especially the pompous ones. There are few Do's-and-Don'ts I follow. I don't care whether or not a butterfly can fly between each flower in a bouquet (since I like them tightly clustered, it would in any case be impossible), I disagree that stems must never cross each other in arrangement bowls – why not, since they can entwine naturally in gardens? Why not use gypsophila (baby's breath) as frosty lace among cut, mixed flowers (roses in particular)? It is much more than just a filler. Great floral masterpieces by medieval painters often include this delicate little flower. Frankly, I am more touched by an armful of garden flowers just placed, as picked, into a proper container than by a bouquet plotted to take care of the mythical butterfly or to worry about measured heights and widths. Are rules everything? No! 'Making Things Up', in my view, is much more fun.

◆

I began to appreciate the art of flower arranging when I was very young. Events which still haunt my memory have crystallized my taste. When I was just a teenager, I was taken by friends to dine with a retired diplomat and his wife who had sharpened their tastes with each foreign post and, on retirement, converted a barn into a highly personal and beautiful home. We entered on a level above an enormous living-room. Looking down, there was a glorious muddle of books, *objets d'art,* comfortable furniture and a roaring fire. But what mattered most in that fascinating room was the one bouquet – only one – on an oversized coffee table set between facing couches before the fireplace. Without fuss, the hostess had piled a vivid mixture of masses of nasturtiums (there could have been hundreds) in reds, yellows and oranges, in a huge copper wash-basin. The flowers danced like added flames.

◆

I didn't realize it then but, in one easy lesson, I had learned the value and the impact of massing flowers – even using the humble nasturtium. I have since done the same with jonquils, buttercups and daisies – plonking an armful of one or the other into simple (often crockery) bowls. I'm happiest when they look as much as possible as they did before being cut. Since they are often crowded in the garden to make a strong statement, doing so indoors gives them an effect as natural as where they grew.

◆

I learned another lesson in London in 1953, as American Ambassador to the Coronation of Queen Elizabeth II. After the ceremony, we were taken to lunch in Westminster Hall. The wine brown walls, darkened by age, had been decorated the previous evening in only two unexpected colours, giving us a shock of delight – I'd never seen mauve flowers teamed with apricot ones! I learned on this historic occasion how beautiful an unconventional coupling of colours could be and I now make it a habit to grow, as well as buy, apricot and mauve flowers to use together.

◆

So don't be afraid to experiment. Invent. Liberate your imagination. Follow intuition. Be natural. Adjust as you go along. And improvise, improvise. Don't be inhibited. You'll be surprised at how creative you prove to be. Mistakes may happen from time to time, but they will nearly always be correctible, and 'winning back' a false start makes the success at the end all the more rewarding.

◆

There's a charming two-word rule for flowers, given to me by Beverley Nichols, the noted gardener and author. He said *'Love them.'* I recommend these words to you.

Dozens of bright red dahlias as I love seeing them: leafless and unadorned, with only their flower buds for accompaniment, packed tightly in a gleaming brass pan. Thoroughly unconventional in terms of traditional flower arranging, but no less beautiful for all that. The dahlias themselves are the star of the show, not the technical prowess of the arranger.

FLORAL POWER

When I was very young, flowers and fairies were inseparable. Children had no doubt that fairies lived in flowers, and slept inside the closed-up petals. They used tiny mushrooms as chairs, larger ones as tables. Such childhood images are not easy to brush aside. Even Lewis Carroll's Alice in *Alice's Adventures in Wonderland* has the same natural affinity to flowers – she always talked with them. Some adults do so even now, insisting that affectionate words keep flowers happy and healthy.

The ancient Greeks and Romans wove flowers into their mythology. Perhaps the best known myth is that of Narcissus, the beautiful youth who fell in love with his own reflection in a forest pool, and died, pining away for this unattainable love. The flowers that grew on the spot where he died were given his name. Daphne, a mountain nymph, was pursued by Apollo whose advances she refused. Trapped by him at last, Daphne called out to Mother Earth in despair and was saved at the last minute by being transformed into a laurel tree. The small, highly scented green flowers of *Daphne laureola* help commemorate this long-ago mythological event. The first hyacinth was said to have sprouted where the blood of the dying youth, Hyacinth, touched the ground. Slain by a jealous would-be lover, Hyacinth lives today as the flowering bulbs we plant in our gardens or 'force' in our homes and greenhouses.

Long after the classical period, flowers were still thought to possess mystical force. In medieval times, daisies were called 'the eyes of God' because it was said that God watched man's every move through the open eyes of the daisy. Culpeper's *Complete Herbal and English Physician* recorded of violets: 'They are fine, pleasing plants of Venus, of a mild nature, in no way harmful'.

THE LANGUAGE OF FLOWERS

As well as being imbued with divine characteristics and commemorating divine events, flowers have become emblems for a vast range of human characteristics and feelings. There is an enchanting little Victorian book which sets out a complete language of flowers: each of several hundred listed plants symbolizes a specific emotion, desire or quality. Narcissus, for example, represented egotism, in deference to the self-love of that mythological youth. Thus, to receive a bunch of narcissi was not in the least complimentary. On the other hand, a bouquet of orange blossom meant, in the eyes of the giver, that your purity equalled your loveliness – a most old-fashioned lover's compliment. Though most roses, are, and always have been, symbols of love, there are no less than 34 meanings attributed to them – according to the colour, type and combination of roses presented (a fully-opened rose placed over two buds, for example, stood for secrecy). The York and Lancaster rose (*Rosa damascena* 'Versicolor') – with its sometimes pink, sometimes white and sometimes two-toned flowers – symbolized war, recalling the English War of the Roses. A white rose and a red rose presented together symbolized unity. The yellow rose was not at all nice to receive, indicating that the affection of the donor was on the wane. Today, it has regained its stature in the Yellow Rose of Texas. A moss rose bud was an unashamed confession of true love. In earlier days there was a double excitement in receiving a bouquet, for even a blade of grass in it was loaded with meaning; all this has been displaced today, in our coldly rational way of life.

In language, however, the symbolism lives on. 'Pure as a lily', 'fresh as a daisy', 'shy as a violet' and 'lovely as a rose' are comparisons as valid today as they were a hundred years ago. And although children's names go in and out of fashion, and always will, babies will continue to be named Lily, Daisy, Violet, Rose, Iris, Daphne and Primrose, as long as flowers are around to provide inspiration.

Today's children are exposed to videos, television, computers and all manner of space-age technology, but still hold up buttercups (as I did as a child) under each other's chins, checking for the bright yellow reflection that reveals a love of butter. Young girls, no matter how sophisticated and urbane, still use the petals of a daisy to find the answer to that age-old question: 'he loves me, he loves me not'. If you want a reassuring answer, start off with 'he loves me'. There is usually an odd number of petals in daisies, so you should end up with the answer 'he loves me', a fact I only recently discovered.

Though the magical and mythological powers of flowers are largely dismissed in today's no-nonsense world, their medicinal powers are regarded by scientists, botanists and pharmaceutical companies with seriousness and respect. The modest rosy periwinkle, for example, is vital for the treatment of certain types of leukaemia (saving four out of five sufferers, where twenty-five years ago only one out of five survived). Heart patients have been helped for years by digitalis, the drug found in foxglove. Some plant-based

John Tenniel's illustration from Lewis Carroll's *Through the Looking Glass* shows Alice deep in conversation with lilies and roses. "'O Tiger-lily!'' said Alice, addressing herself to one that was waving gracefully about in the wind, "I wish you could talk!" "We can talk!", said the Tiger-lily, "when there's anybody worth talking to.'"

The rose-bay willowherb fairy, from *Flower Fairies of the Wayside*, by Cicely Mary Barker. The delightful idea that every flower houses a fairy is a favourite one for children, who have a special affinity to flowers. It is also one more manifestation of the special significance – religious, mythological, symbolic – given to flowers throughout history.

drugs treat mental disorders, and recent scepticism of the thousands of herbal remedies, administered over the centuries for physical and mental complaints, is slowly and steadily disappearing.

But back to the garden: I am saddened by the trend over the last few years of breeding ever larger and larger flowers on ever smaller and smaller plants, This may be because of smaller gardens or perhaps just a frantic determination to get a blaze of colour, no matter how small the patch of ground. Scent and, in some cases, natural grace have suffered; some of the smaller, old-fashioned and heavily scented flowers have been crowded out by their more modern relatives. This is blatantly true of some

Using cut flowers as decoration is almost as universal as domesticity itself, and examples can be found far back into history. The ancient Egyptians were particularly fond of the lotus, the sacred flower of the goddess Isis, and special vases, with several spout-like openings, were designed to hold them. This Roman mosaic, from the second century AD, is an early depiction of mixed flowers, informally grouped in a simple wicker basket. Roses, tulips, morning glories and carnations are among the flowers shown, and its fresh, unstudied appeal is as charming today as it was centuries ago.

sweet peas, of carnations and pinks, and of some of the modern hybrid tea roses. There is one exception close to my heart: the 'Fleur Cowles' rose, bred and named for me by the famous firm of Gregory's of Nottingham, with a pure fragrance; other growers are now gradually learning to bring back the old scented roses.

Flowers are ideal companions. Like us, they *live* – ever changing: buds open, leaves unfurl, colours fade or intensify as flowers and foliage live out their lives. They repay proper care with beauty, and even if you don't look after them properly they die in an uncomplaining way. Even dried flowers and the relatively new and exquisite silk flowers represent life. Though the former are dead and the latter never lived, the imagery of life is so strong that the reality is overlooked. To me, and to many people, flowers in the home are as important as food, and this is true in all walks of life, from the magnate with his staff of gardeners to the cottager working his own plot.

People have always had their own preferences and attachments to flowers. For Disraeli, it was the yellow primrose; Tennyson loved the tiny flowers that grew in crannied stone walls. Dickens was fond of the geranium and Oscar Wilde, the lily. Robert Burns' love was for a red, red rose and Gertrude Stein settled, repetitively, for the species unspecified: 'A rose is a rose is a rose.' Clare Booth Luce, the former American Ambassador, never appeared in

This fifteenth-century painting (*above*), 'The Garden of Paradise', by the Master of the Middle Rhine, uses flowers to bring symbolism as well as beauty to the image. Before the madonna lily (*Lilium candidum*) became widely grown, the iris was the flower of the Virgin, symbolizing chastity and purity.

public without a rose pinned to her suit or dress. And no one has ever seen Douglas Fairbanks Jr. or Prince Bernhard of the Netherlands without a carnation in their respective buttonholes. Queen Elizabeth, the Queen Mother, often wears hats which surround her face with a mass of flowers, like nature's own halo.

I admit, without apology, to a personal prejudice against three flowers (see page 125) but I'm sure most other people also have their dislikes as well as preferences. I dismiss those three *flora non grata* from my mind and concentrate, instead, on the flowers I do like. I have listed these

Seventeenth-century Dutch and Flemish flower paintings combine the scientist's devotion to detail with an exuberant celebration of the subject. The paintings often show idealized combinations of flowers that, in nature, bloom in different seasons. This still life (*right*) is by Jan Davidsz de Heem.

towards the end of the book in my 'Floral Palette'; whether from florist or garden, they are the ones I prefer, love and use. I try to change my combinations of their colours – not doing the same thing over and over again, which would be the floral equivalent of perfecting and serving one or two menus so often your family and guests are bored to tears. Make flower ideas innovative and exciting, instead of learning by rote or basing arrangements solely on past successes.

CHANGING TACK

The universal appeal of flowers is unquestionable. What people do with them once the flowers are cut is quite another matter, and one that is very much open to question and assessment. In traditional flower arranging (which I try to avoid) strictly set out geometrical shapes – the asymmetrical or symmetrical triangle, or the Hogarth curve (rather like a slightly tilted 'S' shape), oval, perpendicular, fan crescent, circle – govern the design and finished look of your arrangement. Each of these basic shapes has been further defined and limited by rules such as proportion, the relationship of one stem to another (in terms of heights or horizontal spread) and the relationship between flowers and the height and width of the container. To me, this approach becomes more like a mathematical problem than an enjoyable response to the flowers at hand.

Ikebana, the Japanese art of flower arranging, calls for an attitude towards flowers that I, as a Westerner, find impossible to accept. It is not my nature to abide by any strict laws such as those of the Ikebana school, which depend upon oriental mysticism, oriental regimentation, oriental religion and the Oriental's disciplined patience. Although I genuinely respect its artistic commitment and ancient origins, Ikebana is too abstract and too intellectual. I prefer the emotional approach.

WILD FLOWERS

This book is about breaking through preconceived notions of flowers and how to use them decoratively. To me, the most sorely underrated and underused of all the flowers are the common wild flowers, the 'weeds' of fields, roadsides and hedgerows. I exclude from this category the rare, endangered and nearly extinct wild flowers and plants, that are rightly protected by law. On pages 141–2 are the latest lists of specially protected American and British plants; you cannot pick, dig up, destroy or collect the seeds from any of these plants, nor can you dig up any other wild plant without the permission of the owner of the land. If you look upon wild flowers as loot for your own garden, give up the thought: wild flowers tend to grow and thrive only where they have chosen to sow themselves. It grieves me to see people dig up foxgloves from roadsides and light woodlands. They are usually biennial plants, which means that they die after flowering and the effort of the floral thief is an entirely wasted one. More importantly, the seeds of the stolen foxgloves are also wasted – which means the loss of future generations of these delightful, graceful and life-saving flowers.

Modest and unprepossessing, masses of buttercups and daisies are accommodated (not arranged!) in a wicker cachepot. Common wild flowers that grow prolifically (perhaps even too prolifically for the farmers' liking) make charming material for indoor displays. The less prolific wild flowers are best enjoyed in the wild, left to grow and multiply and give pleasure to others.

Fortunately, you can now buy wild flower seed from specialist seedsmen, either as mixed wild flowers or single species. Common meadow and woodland wild flowers can be yours to enjoy and pick: violets, cowslips, foxgloves, primroses and wood anemones, for example. And the pleasure is all the greater because no hedgerow, field or woodland has been robbed for your own delight.

Among the sturdiest of wild flowers is the cow parsley, or Queen Anne's lace, which I value perhaps above all other wild flowers (and now grow it in my garden). Its magnificent scale, combined with the delicate and intricate lacy beauty of the flower head, makes it one of the most versatile of all flowers – whether for formal or country-style arrangements (see opposite). On its own or combined with wild or garden flowers, it always looks 'right'. It continues to be pretty when the fresh green seeds replace the lacy white flowers or when, in darkest winter, its gaunt brown skeletal form is all that remains to be added to dried flower arrangements.

Another natural survivor I feel no qualms about picking is the buttercup. Armfuls of these intensely yellow flowers, placed in a simple container without any attempt at 'arranging' them, is the most beautiful way of showing off their charm (as I've done on page 15). Daisies and poppies, which farmers consider unwelcome intruders in their fields, could not be more welcome in my home; likewise the pink and purple clovers that live in pastures and on roadsides. Try, for example, mixing them with small moss roses, or combine clover with wine-red roses.

No matter how you use them, the absolute naturalness of wild flowers will be welcome. Loose stems of wild honey-suckle (in flower or in berry), great arching sprays of black-berry (in flower or in berry), wild thistles with their attractive leaves (beware, they're prickly), and pink, red or purple flower heads – all of these challenge the imagination. They are far more exciting raw material than the poker-straight, almost factory produced, chrysanthemums, available month in, month out, from the florist. The ancestors of many of our most revered garden plants were once wild plants – even weeds – in other parts of the world. Brought back by missionaries, diplomats and explorers, they naturally assumed a precious rarity value. Without belittling the flowers grown in gardens today, I beg you not to let the fact that a flower is wild and free of cost blind you to its inherent beauty.

Often, a carefully chosen and informally presented bunch of wild flowers can mean more than the stiff and somehow anonymous frontal arrangements that come from many florists. Among the royal, rich and famous, to whom florists' flowers are an everyday occurrence, modest bouquets of wild flowers are especially appreciated (as I learned when I once sent such a bouquet, a fat handful of wild liles-of-the-valley, tied in white satin ribbon – for which I still get thanked after many years).

Such posies are memorable because of their uniqueness. An appreciation of wild flowers extends to the not-so-rich urban dwellers, and those ill or bedridden – who will be particularly touched by them. A bunch of bluebells brings to mind the woodlands in spring, and a small bouquet of snowdrops, the woodlands in damp winter.

A froth of cow parsley (also called Queen Anne's lace), lights up a dark, unused fireplace in summer. There are few more humble flowers to be found – cow parsley is neither rare nor expensive, growing freely, as it does, along roadsides and hedgerows. Yet it is one of my all-time favourites, and invaluable for creating a large scale, yet charming and delicate, floral show.

TABLE MANNERS AND ROOM SETS

Cut flowers and foliage are guests in your home and you expect certain things from them. They should be well mannered, interesting and amusing without being over-powering, and they should reflect your taste, personality and character. You should choose them discriminatingly. Try to imagine where they would look best (I never start without a table plan, a room plan, a colour plan). Flowers must go together; they must be chosen with as much care as you take in deciding who to invite to see them.

HIGH RISE

Flowers for the table come high on the list of things I first think about before entertaining. There they will be an inescapable close-up display of your taste, to be looked at and admired (or not). And because guests and flowers are so close, getting the flowers wrong means an instantly visible failure. If you have ever been to a dinner party where the person sitting opposite was totally obscured by the too large, too tall or too pretentious flowers on the table, you'll understand and arrange flowers well above or well below head level. A construction containing too many flowers, piled high, is unfair to guests and absolute death to table conversation.

My favourite solution is the high-rise bouquet. I agree with many people who haven't kind words for crowded, imper-sonal high-rise buildings and high-rise towns, and the high-rise life that results from living there. The high-rise bouquet, however, is as lovely as some high-rise forms are distasteful to live in.

The first high-rise flower table ornaments I ever saw were made for me about thirty-five years ago when I needed ten tables of ten for a bride's dinner dance. 'Don't let the flowers interfere with the view', I requested. The professional designer responded by making balls of white carnations, set on sticks about 1m (3ft) above each table's height. The stems were disguised by satin ribbon, and tied in a bow at the neck of each carnation ball with streamers floating on the table. The bottom stands were weighted down by stones covered in moss. The room looked beautiful.

They were a forerunner to the high rise solution so often used today. I have made a simple variation on this theme on page 21, using red and white carnations and ribbons. In this case, I used a very tall, narrow glass container instead of a pole to achieve the height, not hard to do.

A ball made out of plastic foam and covered with fresh or dried flowers can become the perfect high-rise arrangement if you use it as a 'tree' on a branch or dowel 'trunk'. The basic instructions are given on page 122, and the variations on the theme are as open-ended as your own imagination. You can tie ribbons to the neck of the ball, using colours that complement the flowers and suit the tablecloth. You can cut the ribbon streamers long enough to meet the table and curve gracefully on it. Or you can spray the wooden stems in a colour to match or complement the flowers before weaving them loosely with ivy. Again let the ribbons trail over the table. If you are using ivy to hide or decorate the poles, repeat it with tiny sprigs tucked into the bouquet itself.

I can never resist multiples, and multiple high-rises are no exception. Use a large container — a large clay flowerpot will do — and put two or three carefully chosen leafless branches into it. Each can be painted a different colour, to repeat the colour theme of the flowers you'll use. Make a small ball of flowers to top each stem, using different types of flowers for each ball, or limit yourself to one type of flower — chrysanthemum, rose, dahlia or carnation are good choices — but do each ball in different coloured flowers. Two or three such multiple high-rise arrangements can march down a very long buffet table and I guarantee they will create a memorable impression. Another idea: turn one high rise into a maypole by tying narrow ribbons in several colours to the neck and swirling them round the stem. Or extend the idea further by leading each ribbon to each table setting.

There are other forms of high-rise table decorations besides a floral ball. Try a tall container with cascading plant material. *Euphorbia myrsinites* is one of my favourites; its long willowy stems, pointed greyish leaves and tiny flower bracts are attractive but not invasive when it comes to seeing across the table. Equally stunning and unusual would be a tall glass container filled with the tails of the green form of love-lies-bleeding (*Amaranthus caudatus* 'Viridis'). For me, the green form has an exotic quality, while the red form is simply old-fashioned. The long, beautiful racemes of wisteria are naturally vertical but stubbornly short-lived once cut. (The Japanese put the cut stems into pure alcohol, and follow this with several hours soaking in water, which might be worth trying.) They will last at least one evening, in any case.

Long-stemmed, deep red and white carnations provide the basic ingredient for this lovely high-rise display. Tightly bunch the flowers, then secure them firmly, just under the flower heads, with matching ribbons. Place the stems in a tall, slender and, most importantly, heavy-based, glass vase. High-rise table centrepieces, such as this one, allow your guests to see and talk to one another while dining, without having to fight their way through, over or around huge floral displays.

Previous page
A fireplace mantel in summer makes a stage setting for a parade of wildly different containers, each filled with a single type of flower. The containers range from the rare and expensive to ordinary kitchen ware, and the flowers from modest, communal garden cornflowers, or bachelor's buttons, to florists' carnations. This multiple-vase, multiple-flower approach works equally well on table tops, window sills and even floors. Though restrained, the effect is charming and approachable, exactly what one wants in a home.

Nature provides its own forms of high-rise — delphiniums, hollyhocks, and giant lilies, to name a few, and an umbrella stand in the front hall is a marvellous setting for them. Here, delphiniums (their stems in a concealed waterproof container) bring light and delicacy to the sombre, dark-stained furniture.

For a luncheon, replace the candle in a candlestick with a little water and one large flower head cut off its stem. Depending on the number and type of candlesticks, the effect can be either amusing or resplendent.

With a buffet table (where the problems of cross-table vision and conversation don't exist), you can display the flowers as high and as wide as you like. To be daring, place a tiny table on top of the real one and use it as the framework on which to form your bouquet. Try a tight bouquet of roses resting on top of the tiny table, with delicate sprays of ivy down and on to the buffet table.

Chief among the ready-made high-rise flowers is the so-called giant lily *(Cardiocrinum giganteum)*, with its beautiful, white trumpet-shaped flowers, heart-shaped leaves and extraordinary height (taller than a man). This, I admit, is too tall for a table high rise, but there is no reason why you shouldn't use one giant lily in a firmly balanced container on the floor. Two or three giant lilies, if you are lucky enough to have them available, make an even bolder visual statement. You might consider using one on either side of a window to frame the view outside. There are many true lilies *(Lilium)* that will cheerfully provide a 1m (3ft) high clear stem, and a group of these in a tall, slender container makes an exquisite table-top high rise. On a smaller scale, a single amaryllis plant in its pot does the same trick. Sit it down on a circle of leaves. If the pot is an ordinary plastic one, conceal it in a basket, tie a colourful kerchief around it, or glue leaves to cover it. (I explain how in the chapter on tools and techniques.)

There are places in every home, no matter how small, that call out for a high-rise flower. A dark, dull, empty corner is one — or between the curtains of a window with a bad view. I find that the most dramatic spot is immediately inside the front door, where the flower greets the guests upon arrival and bids them farewell when they leave. The high-rise flowers you may try include the cow parsley (Queen Anne's lace), sunflower, delphinium, rhubarb flower and the magnificent foxtail lily *(Eremurus robustus)*. The latter can equal the giant lily in stature, and its tall stems are covered with pink, trumpet-shaped flowers.

LOW LIFE

There is a table-top alternative to high-rise arrangements which still provides an impressive table centrepiece without obscuring the guests' view of each other: a shallow arrangement of flowers on which your guests can look down. Centrepieces of miniature (but in no way twee) landscapes are delightful. Moss forms the 'lawn'; use bun moss from your garden if you can, or use the sphagnum moss available from the florist. Pack it tightly into a shallow container – pie plate, baking tin or tray – or fix it with toothpicks or hairpins to a shallow block of plastic foam. The vertical edges of the container can be disguised with a nest of pretty leaves or moss attached with glue. Decorate the mossy surface with a collection of short-stemmed flowers. If the table is a long, narrow one, make two 'gardens', one for each end. I once covered a bed of moss (sitting on unseen plastic to protect the tablecloth) with short-cropped white roses (see page 120). It was exquisite on white linen with white porcelain. Tiny, pocket-sized zinnias look lovely embedded in moss, and so do lilies-of-the-valley, short sprigs of rosehips, berries and lichen-covered leafless twigs, each according to the season. Try using a set of ash trays or shallow dishes, each filled with a different mixture of moss, autumn leaves and berries or berries alone. An example of this is shown on page 64, and is a true feast for the eyes.

When using moss, spray it daily with a fine mist of luke-warm water and it should serve you well through several arrangements. When not in use, keep it in a plastic bag in the refrigerator.

You can bring the garden to the table in a more realistic and natural fashion by using small plants, roots and all, for a temporary display. A series of drinking glasses, each one holding a tiny flower bulb – snowdrop, grape hyacinth, miniature narcissus or miniature winter-flowering iris are just a few suggestions – can form an intricately beautiful centrepiece. The plants can be replanted when the party is over. On a large scale, lift a group of pansies, with soil clinging to the roots, and display them 'growing' in a shallow glass cooking pan, leaves tumbling over. Moss can hide the surface soil if necessary.

If you are feeling creative (and ambitious), try making a bird's nest centrepiece. Start with twigs and moss, and build it up to a round, hollow shape as best you can. Don't aim for perfection, because real nests are never precisely geometrical or firm. Fill the centre with sprigs of various flowers in a concealed container. Nesting is a spring activity, and I enjoy making an equally spring-like display: aubrieta, alyssum, forget-me-nots, double daisies, primroses, polyanthus and wallflowers.

Incidentally, may I urge you to cultivate the friendship of your local florist. You should then be able to buy a few of several different kinds of flowers, rather than a whole bunch of each. A mixture of flowers is the basis for the above display, and just as pretty as flowers of a single sort.

A 'low-life' display with a touch of humour. Spotlessly clean, clay flower pots are lined with aluminium foil and filled with earth. A different cut flower is 'planted' in each one and the pots are marched down the centre of the table. This pleasantly bizarre floral fantasy contrasts with the formality of the setting – white linen, bone china and silver – and helps take the 'edge' off the occasion.

Another low-life idea dependent on a mixture of flowers is one I saw on the table of Baron Philippe de Rothschild's home in Mouton. Different, very small receptacles (in this case valuable antiques) were filled with soil and one solitary cut flower 'planted' in each. Don't be deterred by lack of antique containers; in the photograph above I used little clay flowerpots instead.

FACES ONLY

I have a passion for 'faces only' on a table, which means using little more than the flower heads. There is nothing wrong with enhancing the flowers by close-ups of their heads. Looking down on them in low containers means there is nothing to distract you from the beauty of the flowers. They are my favourite form of low-life display although I suspect that the too-traditional florist or flower arranger would pale at the thought of decapitating flowers so near their heads. Long-stemmed flowers are highly valued because of their height, but my own philosophy is quite different: I prefer to look down into the face of a flower. A huge sunflower head in a shallow soup plate is absolutely stunning. Use a soup plate slightly smaller than the incredibly detailed sunflower, so you don't see the edge of the plate beneath.

Show the faces of paeonies in champagne glasses. Sit each flower on top of the rim, with its stem in water and its petals hanging over, as shown on page 29. Try dahlias and large chrysanthemums, as the seasons change — always remembering to hide the rim of the glass with the outer petals. In South Africa, I once looked down on three vivid amaryllis heads which had been cut from their stalks. It would take courage to do this in a temperate climate, where they are cosseted as plants, but in South Africa and Brazil they grow wild and are as easily available as our native cow parsley (Queen Anne's lace). The trumpet-shaped flowers from just one lily would give the same effect. Also trumpet-shaped are the small blue flowers of the heads of agapanthus, another treasure of South African origin. Like the amaryllis, it can be used high-rise style, or as a face only (with leaves as a trimming). Rest a single head on a champagne glass or use several heads tucked in a moss bed or on a very large ash tray. Fortunately, agapanthus grows well in sunny, sheltered borders in temperate climates, so they can be used with a slightly more lavish and generous hand.

The exquisite and miraculously formed passion flower is another world traveller. From South America, it has made its way to sunny gardens on every continent. Use its intricate flower heads (said to symbolize the various elements of the Crucifixion) as I have used clematis (see page 104). Interestingly, passion flowers last longer as 'faces only' than they do when displayed on their trailing stems.

The camellia is winter's almost perfect flower and the almost perfect flower for face-only use. Carefully detach one and float it in a small glass. Stand it on its own enamel-like dark green leaves or float several flowers in a pure

Pansy faces — fresh, unpretentious and charming — are among my favourites, and I never tire of setting them out in all their different possible colour combinations. Here are bright yellow and rich, rust-red pansies arranged in circles in a shallow dish. A small ramekin in the centre holds a slightly raised bouquet. It is easiest to work from the middle outwards.

white porcelain bowl, surrounded by the same shining leaves. The summer equivalent is the water lily, a natural for a floating display. Because they open and close in response to the light, you may find that they have shut their petals once indoors. Dropping melted wax between each petal will keep the flower open. You can artificially recreate their natural environment by placing a layer of pebbles in the bottom of the shallow, water-filled container. Looking down upon the open lily, floating above clear water and a pebbly bottom, is like looking into a lily pond in miniature.

Being able to observe closely the intensely blue faces of gentians (*above*) is a special treat, particularly on this grand scale. They are tightly packed in a shallow marble bowl, which in no way competes with the 'stars of the show', but provides a cool and sophisticated setting.

Water lilies are as difficult to come by as they are exquisite, and you can instead float one beautiful plump iris by itself in a glass or in a parade of glasses, each containing a single iris. One iris at a small table set for two makes a change from the more usual rose, and none of the romance will be lost. I float the cosy little campanulas in water, too, picking off dozens of blossoms one by one from the stems. The biennial Canterbury bell (*Campanula medium*) is sometimes called the cup-and-saucer flower. Their large pink white or blue cup flowers also become perfect 'boats' to float on a tiny table-top lake.

Faces on a larger scale, this time, but equally beautiful. Each paeony (*opposite*) is resting in its own wine glass, the rim hidden by petals. While leaves would have detracted from the exquisite, over-all pattern of gentians (*above*), here they are used to add contrast.

Single flower faces are always dramatic, but you can play with crowds of faces, too. Bunch and tie together enough French marigolds to make one large, composite one, leafless and richly coloured, and float it in your container. I also like to arrange zinnia faces the same way – in low, tight, concentric circles, starting with one colour for the centre, another to surround it and a third to form the frame. The result is stunning; you can still see each face and yet together they became a single, hugely dramatic, fantasy flower head.

A perfect example of a 'low life' table arrangement: guests can enjoy the flowers and each other's company at the same time. Here, inexpensive blue church glass is teamed up with yellow, with stunning results.

Any combination of flowers can be used, but keep in mind the colour of the linen and china.

The small, deep-blue glasses obtainable from religious supply stores (conventionally used to hold candles) can each be filled with a tight bunch of one type of flower – anemones, sweet peas, sweet Williams, miniature tulips or rosebuds. Stack the flower-filled glasses close together in a large, low basket, for a multiple display (see page 124). The effect, a mosaic of flower faces, is similar in feeling to a *mille-fleur* paperweight. I made this the first time with wild flowers in Greece, to give to the late Queen Frederika – and she preferred them to other massive, and more formal, birthday flower arrangements.

HIGH DRAMA

The most dramatic use I have ever made of flowers was on an occasion in Denmark, many years ago, when I learned the art of furnishing with flowers – a valuable experience that I would not wish to repeat. My friend Victor Borge had purchased a Danish castle (formerly the home of the last English Queen of Denmark) called Friedenlund. I helped him write the plans and instructions which were issued to decorate completely its interior. A month before the expected date of completion, dinner invitations were sent to Denmark's Prime Minister, the American Ambassador to Denmark and the Danish Ambassador to the United States and to us, to celebrate what was to be the re-opening of a fully renovated and furnished castle. My husband and I were met at the airport, two days before the dinner party, by a crestfallen, almost tearful Mr Borge.

'Nothing has been finished! The castle is completely empty! What shall we do?'

There wasn't time to panic; something inventive had to be done, and instantly. Barest essentials were hired: a cook and waiter, enough furniture to seat eight people, two trestle tables, dishes, utensils, pots and dining chairs. The drawing-room presented an incredible problem; it was circular in shape, with a diameter of 15m (50ft). I decided to attempt a stage set. Hundreds of metres of white sheeting were wildly swathed around the full-length windows which looked out on the lawns. I then sent my husband off to buy the entire contents of two flower shops – something every man must dream of doing!

The flowers were massed in every conceivable container, the hideous ones hidden by others. Flowers were banked in and around the windows with rented spotlights focusing on them in the falling dusk. In the dining-room, we draped the trestle dining-table and the trestle serving table in more of the white sheeting, pinning garlands to both.

The evening, so lavishly focussed on flowers, was a complete success. If guests missed conventional furniture and decor, they never questioned the eccentric substitutions. The food was good, the conversation good, and Victor Borge never funnier.

While I never again expect to use flowers on that grand scale (and with such a frenzied race against the clock), the story makes a valid point. Where you place flowers in a room, how you light and mass them, and what you surround them with, is what counts.

Don't overlook windows; they make a natural stage for

flowers. The back lighting they provide does wonders for a huge display of dried flowers, for example. The less attractive the view, the more it can be concealed by flowers and foliage. If the view is a lovely one, just dress the windowsill with small potted plants or containers with flowers. Try the visual pun of repeating on a windowsill *indoors* a row of the same geraniums in the window box *outdoors* – the boundary between indoors and outdoors vanishes! On the floor in front of a full-length window, try a row of brightly coloured cineraria plants, and the window immediately becomes the room's focal point.

Fireplaces provide another instant stage setting. In spring and summer, replace the logs with flowers. I fill an empty grate with delphiniums and ferns, with cow parsley (Queen Anne's lace) as on page 17, or with a large tub of leaves punctuated by one or two flowers (it is the ideal spot for silk flowers if the fireplace isn't blocked, as draughts from the chimney will shorten the lives of real flowers). And don't forget mantelpieces. Their narrow width is a challenge that can be met with small, flower-filled containers displayed single file, as shown on page 18.

Parade a collection of different flowers in pots on the floor in front of the empty grate in summer, or fill a log basket with a glorious mixture of garden flowers to place in front of, not alongside, the fireplace.

The floor can be another great and unexpected place for flowers – a large bowl with foliage and flowers, or flowers or foliage alone can be placed next to a couch. If a pair of couches face each other, have two containers to more than double the effect. Use common sense, though: a container that is small and not easily noticed is likely to be knocked over, as is one put right on a definite 'route' from one room to another. Even those in relatively safe spots should be heavy enough to remain upright after the occasional, unintentional knock. Safest of all is a basket weighted down with sand or stone and filled with flowers as a floral doorstop, an arrangement I use in my country home.

The use of mirrors is an old trick; flowers and foliage are visually doubled and any arrangement, however modest or grand, becomes a twin. Shelves in front of a mirror are the place to parade a collection of tiny containers. I have used Lalique glass bottles this way, each one containing a single stem, alternately, of pink and white long-tendrilled moth orchids *(Phalaenopsis)*. Not everyone has access to Lalique glass or exotic orchids, but the idea can be carried out in more modest materials.

Very often modern rooms are neutral in colour – all white, white and black, indefinable grey or beige – and usually call

The rigidly geometric form and style of this white abstract painting have been heightened and echoed by the white geometric vase directly beneath it. The red carnations, which repeat the only 'colour' in the painting, have lost some of their individuality as flowers and have taken on a textural, abstract quality as well.

for drama. Every piece of furniture, every painting has been placed with the single-mindedness of a perfectionist; there is no place for half-thought-out floral ideas. The photograph above illustrates the point: no vast expenditure was called for, but a great deal of thought gave the few flowers dramatic importance.

Modern interiors, with their spaciousness and often blank walls, are perfect settings for high-rise flowers, a single, tall blue agapanthus against a white wall, for instance, or a single, well-placed white lily. Leafless winter branches, such as those of magnolia, alder or corkscrew hazel (*Corylus avellana* 'Contorta'), take on the abstract quality of a modern sculpture in a modern setting, and the larger the branch, the more dramatic the display.

There is a special place for black flowers in austere modern interiors. Try one so-called 'black' tulip in a dead-white bud vase, or a tight bunch of the very nearly black form of scabious, all cut to the same height. Visually riveting rather than classically pretty, these black flowers are both natural and unnatural-looking at the same time – ideal focal points in a contemporary setting.

This tablecloth of leaves is for a special occasion only, and one for which you have plenty of extra time, or willing assistants, to help. Start with inexpensive cotton sheeting or a paper tablecloth, pins or glue and tough, large leaves, such as bergenia – used here – or *Fatsia japonica* or *galax*. Starting from the centre, pin down a circle of leaves. Gradually add overlapping layers of leaves, slipping each one under the edge of the circle until you have finished. Glue or pin them in position as you go. When you come to the rim of the table, you may find you need to put a few unseen stitches in the leaves that go over the edge, to make sure they fold neatly and stay in place. Here the leaves nearest the centre have been lifted up a little to hide the container holding the floral centrepiece. Not tricky, but time consuming and certainly worth the effort!

OCCASIONAL CHARM

Throughout the year such occasions as Christmas, Thanksgiving and Easter demand some floral originality. If you are faced with wedding receptions, summer buffets, even picnics and patriotic holidays, they call for something out of the ordinary. Don't panic. Don't just ring your florist to order a *fait accompli* arrangement. Consider instead the fun of doing some of the ideas set out here as inspiration for your own imagination.

For a special summer occasion (a buffet engagement party), I once arranged a separate table just to accommodate desserts, and made the tablecloth entirely of leaves (like the one above). This is not as difficult as it sounds, though somewhat time-consuming. You only need a drop of 25cm (10in) from the table top; but if you were feeling very ambitious you could make an absolutely spectacular table-cloth of leaves reaching down to the floor.

Your choice of treatment of tablecloths – not necessarily such extravagantly leafy ones – should be as carefully considered as the flowers and foliage you are going to use as decoration. Fine damask and linen can never be faulted, but try matching the feeling of the flowers more imaginatively by using an old paisley shawl for an unexpected but beautiful tablecloth, as background for dark flowers and

The pastel blue, mauve, cream and green of the furnishing fabrics are matched – not challenged or over-ruled – by the delicate display of scabious in Victorian Parian vases. The papery flowers, and their enchanting green flower buds, peep out from every conceivable direction, and the arrangement of vases, from short to tall, ensures the maximum floral impact.

autumn foliage. For a harvest festival, why not a cotton patchwork quilt, or ready-quilted cotton fabric? Tuck flowers, foliage and berries into two foam cones or fill a narrow bread basket with ivy and chrysanthemums that pick up the colouring of the quilts. Cutlery which has coloured porcelain, pottery or plastic handles would complete the picture – sometimes flowers can even match them. Gingham may not be immensely innovative when it

Nothing is as elegant as a study in whites: white lilies, white brickwork, white glass and white linen. The translucence of the flowers against the rough brickwork is dependent on strong, direct lighting for its effect, and the green buds and leaves help to 'anchor' the display visually.

comes to tablecloths, but I never fail to find it refreshingly informal – whether deep rust or tawny brown and white checks for autumn, pale blue, yellow or pink and white for spring and summer, or black and white for sophistication. Gingham is inexpensive yet invaluable. I often use gingham napkins to line loosely-woven baskets – with flower-filled containers inside – mixing or matching the gingham colours as I please.

To lift white linen out of the realm of the predictable, I suggest you combine it with a tightly packed bowl of leaf-less white philadelphus – the heavenly scented, mock orange. I once displayed them in a small block of ice formed between two containers, one smaller and stacked inside the other. This sounds difficult; it is not, but it does require

For a wedding or a birthday, let the cakes themselves be the centrepiece, but in a refreshingly informal way. A pale pink tablecloth forms the background, and a deeper pink rosebud decorates each of the three white-iced cakes. Dozens of fresh rose petals complete the picture. Wait until the last possible moment before putting the petals in position, as they could wilt quickly.

two matching cake or bread baking tins, one at least 5cm (2in) larger then the other. Place the smaller one in the centre of the larger, fill the space between the two tins with water and put the two in the freezer for a few hours. A cloth wrung out in hot water is wrapped around the outside one, and you'll find it slips away from the ice; then fill the smaller tin with warm water to remove it. Flowers can be arranged inside the cavity in the resulting ice block. The ice won't melt for hours and can be put on a cookie tin on the table. Cover any of its exposed metal with leaves or moss. There is nothing so elegant and sophisticated as well chosen white-on-pure-white (although poorly chosen white-on-white can look boring or even institutional). The dead white of commercially grown chrysanthemums or carnations, in certain surroundings, can sometimes appear flat but the translucence of white snowdrops, tinged very lightly with green, is another story. I love white lilies against white (see the photograph on page 36), and white lilacs are always welcome in my home for their intricacy as well as their scent. White orchids are high style, white daisies fresh-faced and charmingly old-fashioned. The white-on-white of white wedding cakes on white linen can happily accommodate white flowers, provided they are chosen with care. However, I like to ring the changes with slightly opened fat pink rosebuds, one on each of two white-iced wedding cakes, and then scatter petals on the tablecloth around them, as shown on page 37.

For a national holiday, why not do the national colours in flowers for the table centrepiece? The red, white and blue stripes, shown opposite, were easily made by packing tiny flowers in a bed of plastic foam in a shallow baking pan. The result is an obvious bow to a patriotic occasion.

Red and green mean Christmas. There are so many plants traditionally associated with this holiday (the conifers, holly, ivy, mistletoe and poinsettia) that the raw material is already set out for you. And the traditional ways in which these materials are used – as wreaths, decorated trees, swags and garlands – seem fresh and new every year, in spite of their repeat performances. Still, I do enjoy experimenting, and here are a few suggestions: 'light up' a potted bay tree with red berries, red and white flowers, red and white ribbons fixed singly or in neat little bunches to the branches. Fit the flower stems into florists' vials, which can then be tucked discreetly amid the tree's foliage. A pair of bay trees is admittedly extravagant – but stunning (see page 68). The idea is just as good applied to a miniature bay tree to use on a table.

Shape a cone of plastic foam for a centrepiece, cover it with chicken wire, then pack it tightly with sprigs of holly. The berries will provide all the decoration that is needed, though it is improved by tying a wide red velvet bow at the base. Try wiring a similar cone with massed paper-wrapped Christmas candies, so that every bit of the cone is hidden. Tie a red velvet ribbon to the base and place on a bed of holly. I use this ultimately edible 'sweet' tree for

To celebrate a national holiday – this one could be American, French or English – make the most of patriotic colours. The red cutlery and red, white and blue tablecloth and flowers call for more forethought and imagination than money. Red geraniums, white sweet Williams and blue cornflowers, or bachelor's buttons, were used for this 'flag', but any small flowers in the appropriate colour are fine.

children at Christmas, but it never fails to intrigue adults. Another table-top Christmas tree is a variation on the high-rise, flower-ball theme. Stand a slim but strong branch of a tree, cut to a suitable length, in a large clay flowerpot and pack heavy stones round it to keep it firmly in position. Fix a chicken wire-covered plastic foam ball to the top of the branch using strong wire. Tuck in short sprigs of holly until the surface of the ball is packed solid. For finishing touches, reflective Christmas balls can be added to it if you wish.

Christmas roses *(Helleborus niger)* don't always flower in time for Christmas, especially if the winter has been a cold one, but I've found that protecting them in my garden with a large pane of glass placed over the clump gives the extra warmth they need to flower when I want them most. At Christmas, I mix them with holly and mistletoe for the table. For a most unusual centrepiece fix assorted pebbles to a tray with plasticine, then tuck in bits of foam so you can fill any spaces between the pebbles with berries and white Christmas roses.

EDIBLE DELIGHTS

The marketplace, full of fruit and vegetables, can be as exciting as the best garden. To me, and to many others, the masses of colours and shapes are as beautiful as flowers. The three are at last now allowed to be used together. In fact, I sometimes get more exciting results with all three than with any one on its own.

The Victorians accepted fruit as decoration by using many-tiered epergnes at the dining-table, alternating a layer of fruit with one of flowers. Today, such old-fashioned rules and regulations are gone. Our new attitudes toward informality and fresh ideas have made deliberate combinations of fruit or vegetables with flowers not only acceptable but chic. By this, I don't mean the traditional precarious column of tightly packed fruit and flowers, crowned with a pineapple and held together with pins, wires, dowels and, occasionally, nails. Such self-conscious arrangements and rigid rules of proportion made one distinctly ill at ease. Put to one side all preconceived notions about what you should and should not do: the rest will follow easily.

CABBAGES AND KINGS

Among vegetables, there is nothing less pretentious than the cabbage. I find it absolutely delicious, and I will never forgive Cassandra of London's *Daily Mirror*, who once compared it to steamed, coarse newsprint, probably after being served it watery and overcooked. Mistaken notions of snobbery should not prevent you from serving it, lightly cooked and drained, to the most discerning guests – or from using it to decorate the table. Try putting a small head of wine-red cabbage in a low, hidden bowl, opening the outer leaves of the cabbage to form a frame and hide the bowl. Cut a small opening in the centre of the cabbage, insert a water-filled glass – and finally, one fat pink, fully opened rose. Change the colour combinations to suit the season, your decor, or simply your mood. Try a pale green cabbage with a pink rose (a still life I often paint), a purple cabbage with a deep red rose or a crinkly savoy with pure white roses. Or you could surround a pale green cabbage with pale pink roses in a low, water-filled container.

Without casting aspersions on the kitchen cabbage, there are ornamental kales and cabbages you can grow or occasionally buy, with superb tinted leaves. If you have room to grow a row of mixed ornamental cabbages, you'll have a long supply of cherry-red, pink and creamy-white leaves, in many flower-like patterns. The ordinary dark green cabbage also looks beautiful on its own when framed by white phlox or rhododendron. For a more conventional arrangement try scooping out the centre of a large cabbage (save it for cooking) and carefully filling the shell with such colourful fresh vegetables as red and green chillies, freshly shelled peas and tiny cherry tomatoes. Or make a circular pattern on a large shallow plate, using a cabbage as a centrepiece, then surround it with a ring of globe artichokes or bunches of broccoli.

Broccoli, cabbage's slightly more sophisticated cousin, makes pretty, unusual 'foliage' for bright red geraniums and white daisies. You can even decorate the table with broccoli in bunched 'bouquets' tied with ribbon.

A timely bit of advice when using cabbage and other members of the brassica family decoratively: give the vegetables a good soaking in cold water in a dark place to minimize the risk of a cabbagy smell.

FRUITFUL IDEAS

There are few flowers that can compete with the exquisitely clean and clear yellow of the lemon, and it has long been a favourite of mine for arrangements. I usually fill a French wire basket for shaking washed lettuce with lemons, piled high. For contrast, I tuck in sprigs of glossy dark ivy and finish off with yellow-centred, white daisies. On page 46 I have made a similar arrangement in a wire egg rack. It is an amusing idea for a hot summer's day, whether for a luncheon or a dinner party – elegant but marvellously unpretentious.

Likewise grapes. These fashioned from glass and semi-precious stones have adorned the wealthiest tables, but I don't think they hold a candle to the real thing. A wicker basket of plum-coloured grapes is even more handsome when punctuated with small white flowers. Anemones, too, are ravishing with grapes. Make green grapes the heart of an all-green centrepiece; add green plums, green apples, green pears and green figs. They should be arranged with as much care as any all-flower arrangement. If you still feel the need for flowers, try to maintain the green theme by adding a few exquisite green coral bells: *Heuchera cylindrica* 'Chartreuse' or 'Greenfinch'. Far more common and equally effective are the tiny green star-like flowers of lady's mantle *(Alchemilla mollis).* For more massive floral impact, add the clear green zinnia 'Envy' – stunning.

There is no reason why you shouldn't use fruit as

Previous page
The kitchen, kitchen garden and supermarket hold untapped resources for decorating with flowers. A halved watermelon, for example, makes a natural vase for sweet peas, the pink of one reflecting the pink of the other. Try canteloupe melons with cottage-garden flowers or pale orange roses, or green-fleshed melons with a pretty bouquet of green leaves and white flowers. Pumpkins and marigolds would make a charming autumnal combination.

Scoop out the seeds and a bit of the central flesh, if necessary, being careful to leave a thick rim. Wedge a piece of soaked plastic foam in the centre, then add the flowers, keeping them densely packed near the surface to conceal the foam.

A jovial pun on 'cabbage rose'. Three cabbages – white, green and ornamental – form a framework of display for contrasting roses. Keep the roses fresh by inserting the stems in florists' vials, making a hole in the cabbage with a sharp knife, if necessary.

containers for flowers. Scoop out the lovely orange flesh of canteloupe, for example, and hide a small water-filled container in the shell. With 'country' flowers like daisies or alyssum, the ribbed shell will be a feast for the eyes, and as refreshing as the fruit salad that should accompany it. A watermelon, halved, can have its centre filled with sweet peas (see page 40). In fact the flesh can act as a substitute for wet plastic foam supporting the stems of the sweet peas you stick in.

Take one or two pairs of apples and slice a sliver of flesh from the bottoms to make a firm base (protecting the table with a small piece of clear plastic which you disguise with a layer of glossy leaves). Next, carefully core the fruit and insert a tiny florists' vial of water in the centre of each. This can hold one large flower – a perfect dahlia, perhaps, or a dark red rose, or a spray of white sweet William, or a mass of other tiny flowers such as forget-me-nots or baby's breath *(Gypsophila)*. In the winter, add a spray of red-berried holly, ivy with its black berries, or mistletoe with its translucent and magical white ones. Idea: put a flower-filled apple or pear at each place setting, as a personal posy for your guests.

On a larger scale, cut a sliver from the base of a pumpkin, sit it on a larger, but shallow, water-filled dish. Pile nasturtiums and then the flower heads of orange calendulas (sometimes called pot marigolds by old-fashioned gardeners) thickly around the pumpkin. You might even add tiny sprigs of yellow cherry tomatoes. Or scoop out the centre of a pumpkin (use it for pumpkin pie) and fill the hollow with yellow carnations or chrysanthemums.

The pineapple has been the traditional top for huge arrangements of fruit, but why not try ringing the changes by taking its top off? Replace the leaves and 5cm (2in) of scooped-out pulp with small bunches of pale green grapes, a few seasonal flowers and, finally, some trailing stems of small-leafed ivy (I particularly like the cultivated ivy 'Goldheart', with its bright yellow-centred leaves, or the creamy grey, green and white-leafed 'Glacier'). If you are faced with a pineapple whose leaves have started to go brown at the tips, the combination of 'infill' fruit, flowers and foliage is the perfect solution. Use toothpicks to secure the fruit and foliage in position. The scooped out pineapple, cut into chunks, is delicious with vanilla ice cream.

Many vegetables are, strictly speaking, fruit, because they contain the seeds of future plants. Tomatoes, green peppers and eggplants (or aubergines) fall into this category; so do avocados. Tomatoes come in as many shapes, sizes and colours as some flowers do, and should certainly be accorded the same creative thought. Round and plum-shaped, or squat and irregular, red, yellow, green or splashed and striped with several colours, and ranging in size from huge to tiny, they can be used as containers or in containers. Try hollowing out a large tomato to fill with the distinctively star-shaped, yellow flowers (if you still have any at that stage) from the same tomato plant. The leaves, though not particularly beautiful, have a gorgeous aroma when rubbed between the fingers – worth including on that account alone. Even the 'grubby' square baskets in which soft fruit is sometimes sold can be used to hold cherry tomatoes with yellow daisies, chrysanthemums, rudbeckias, anthemis or coreopsis. The baskets can either be sprayed in colours or used as they come for an intentionally modest effect. Other ideas: round, fat tomatoes punctuated by French marigolds, red peppers with cherry tomatoes and, lastly, a wire basket filled with the perfect, clean red forms of tomatoes with no other accompaniment. The shiny, blue-black skin of aubergine, or eggplant, requires flowers of equally intense colour. I find that the De Caen anemones, with their brilliant colours and black centres, are the most exciting companions. Halve and slightly hollow out the aubergines, then fill each one with water or wet foam and anemones (of one colour or mixed). You might use them like the apples and pears – one at each place setting – or use several aubergines *en masse* as a centrepiece, each one filled with a small clump of mixed flowers. The glistening, leathery skin of avocado makes a good foil for miniature dahlias. Again, halve the fruit, remove the stone, then fill the centre hollow with water or plastic foam and flowers. If done carefully, the avocado can later be diced to add to a salad.

Mushrooms are fruiting bodies, too, and should not be forgotten. White button mushrooms combine charmingly with daisies, miniature zinnias, or tiny pompon chrysanthemums. Many wild mushrooms can provide their own colour. Living in the country, I once collected a few red

Freshly shelled and uncooked garden peas make a perfect foil for pale-pink rosebuds. The peas help to offset the stiffly formal connotations of polished wood, silver and florists' roses. A humorous idea, perhaps, but humour has a rightful place in flower arranging. On a more immediate note, the peas give a foretaste of the meal to come. Put the rosebud stems in florists' vials, and pile the peas onto the dish where it is to be displayed to avoid spilling peas *en route*.

A tiered wire egg basket provides the structural support for this simple arrangement of lemons and variegated ivy. The yellow picks up the colour scheme of the china, linen and cutlery, while the green leaves add contrast and help obscure the wire framework.

mushrooms and put them in a wooden strawberry box, surrounded by fresh watercress – definitely inedible (probably poisonous), yet a flight of fancy which the guests enjoyed. The bright yellow-orange of freshly picked *chanterelles* rivals that of any marigold; display them on a bed of chestnut leaves or moss in a shallow wicker basket. *Chanterelles,* of course, are absolutely delicious to eat, but unless you are certain in your identification of wild fungi, use them for decorations only.

Peppers – green, red or yellow – are often stuffed with meat or rice. Instead try 'stuffing' them with flowers. Nasturtiums overflowing red or yellow peppers make a charming centrepiece: so do green peppers filled with cool white daisies. Cucumbers and courgettes (or zucchini) make long, boat-shaped containers for any small flowers you would like to select. Carefully scoop out the flesh from the centre, taking care not to pierce the skin.

Perhaps the most exciting centrepiece of all can be made of raw asparagus (see page 51). Cover a container with spears of upright asparagus using double-sided sticky tape and then fill it with loosely arranged flowers: I used white daisies. I then heightened the effect by encircling the asparagus with a pale green apple, a green pepper and an avocado – each scooped out to house shortened stems of the same daisies. For a big splash of colour, fill the asparagus-covered container with enough mixed tulips to make a loose, curving arrangement and put one tulip in each of the encircling fruits.

LEAFY GREENS

As if asparagus in its edible state weren't luxury enough, the plant has yet more treats in store for those who seek exciting decorative material. The tender young shoots that appear in May are followed by masses of ferny foliage which is simply the shoots left to grow. In autumn, the frothy mass of foliage turns bright yellow and the female plants bear equally bright, but red, berries. I've packed this 'fern' tightly in a bowl and clipped it to form a ball. Other berries can be added; rosehips are especially pretty. Use the fern in its green form as a background for other foliage or flowers, or massed on its own. Remember that it is closely related to all the other asparagus ferns, including the one most often used by florists, *Asparagus plumosus.* Even smilax *(Asparagus medeoloides)* is a distant cousin, more often seen in America than in British florists' shops.

Salad vegetables – lettuce, watercress, endive, chicory and radicchio – are often overlooked as suitable candidates for arrangements. The brilliant purple colour of radicchio is much loved by *nouvelle cuisine* chefs, who use it sparingly as a garnish for all sorts of dishes; but why not think of it as a 'hem' for a tightly packed bunch of deep red roses? As far as the greens go, few can match the fresh colour of watercress when used as a ruffle around a tightly packed display of spring flowers or, more unusually, around a mound of shiny tangerines or kumquats. Curly green endive is as frilled and delicate as lace and its gradations of colour – dark green round the edge, pure white in the blanched centre – make a perfect showcase in which to display a few small but perfect blooms. Pale pink rosebuds, old-fashioned (and deliciously scented) garden pinks, even individual blossoms of dwarf gladioli tucked in amongst the leaves would be my choice, but have the fun of experimenting yourself with readily available flowers.

I use globe artichoke leaves – a lovely shade of silver grey – as a foil to white summer flowers (checking them first for garden insects which a bath in water will reveal).

Most herbs have tiny, insignificant flowers (the *Umbelliferae* family excepted, but more of these later). What herbs lack in flowers they more than make up for with their fragrance and unpretentious charm. A huge bunch of freshly picked mixed herbs displayed in a shallow wicker basket is not a second-best substitute for flowers but a highly imaginative alternative. And herbs aren't always green. There is a basil as purple as the deepest purple rose, and sages with dusky purple leaves, leaves splashed with gold and grey, and the form 'Tricolor' with grey-green, pink, crimson and creamy-white variegated leaves. There is a bronze-leaved fennel, a lemon balm with leaves splashed bright yellow and deep green, and all sorts of variegated mints. This is not meant to disparage the green herbs: curly-leafed parsley, shiny bay and wild mint, to name a few of my favourites. They are far superior to the dried-up bits of evergreen (why do so many florists automatically include them in bouquets?) and can be used as a complementary foil to flowers. Tuck sprigs of rosemary into mixed arrangements to fill the air with that evocative Mediterranean scent. I once saw a sprig of rosemary placed in a glass of red wine, a beautiful fleeting image. The sprig was removed, of course, before the wine was drunk, but the combination of the deep, deep red and the misty grey was so magical that I will always remember it.

Herbs, on their own or mixed with fruit, flowers or vegetables, can be used as the centrepiece at luncheon or dinner; try some of the herbs used in the dishes you are serving. Freshly chopped mint on new potatoes can be matched by huge bunches of mint in a bowl spiked with a

Nothing could be simpler than a glass dish filled with fresh cherries and daisies, and nothing could more epitomize the joys of summer. To keep the daisies fresh, insert their stems in florists' vials.

few wild flowers or rosebuds, or with their own modest, pale mauve flowers providing the only additional colour. And if your herb garden is confined to a row of small flowerpots on your kitchen windowsill, make the most of what you have. Pack the pots together in a large basket or trug, and weave long stems of ivy around and between the pots. Let some of the ivy trail over the edge of the container and onto the table. When the party is over, return the potted herbs to their sunny windowsill 'garden'.

FLORAL FOOD

The globe artichoke is one of the few flowers we eat, and this highly eccentric vegetable ranks with asparagus in terms of its delicacy and desirability. In Italy, the developing buds can be bought when tiny and tender enough to be eaten raw, but normally it is the nearly mature buds that are cooked and served with a dressing, or occasionally stuffed. The flowers that follow on after are beautiful giant thistle flowers, a splash of mauve. If you can spare two or three from cutting, allow them to mature and then display these in a strong container; I use a tall, black lacquer tumbler. Or make a wheel of the raw artichokes (nearly mature ones can be cooked the next day); fill the spaces between with wide-open red tulips.

Not all herbs have small, modest flowers. The main exceptions are members of the *Umbelliferae* family – dill, fennel and angelica. Their large, flat heads are made up of many tiny flowers, usually in white, yellow or fresh green. Stalks of fennel make a starkly modern, architectural display; cut short, and used as lace round tightly packed roses, the flowers have a Victorian look.

Consider the rhubarb. Though used as a fruit in the kitchen, it is botanically a vegetable (the leaf stalk is the bit that is eaten). What interests me just as much is the flower. It is an enormous heavy one, impressive rather than beautiful, which saps the plant of vigour (traditionally, the developing flower buds are nipped out first). Just one rhubarb flower makes a very bold display, but it does need a container as enormous as itself. Another idea: try using just the huge rhubarb leaves to balance a tall arrangement.

If you grow your own courgettes (or zucchini), you'll have the luxury of harvesting them while still tiny, with their brilliant orange-gold flowers still attached. Pack them upright into a straight-sided glass container for an 'instant' flower and vegetable centrepiece. You can cook the courgettes later, and dip the flowers in batter and deep-fry them, Italian style.

Runner beans, native to South America, were originally

Green vegetables in variety are combined with an equally wide range of white flowers for this impressive centrepiece. Double-sided tape is used to attach asparagus to an inner container – in this case a one-pound size coffee tin – filled with chrysanthemums. Avocados, sliced across the top and slightly scooped out, contain small carnations. Similarly sliced green peppers hold Brompton stock, and a globe artichoke is topped with a single clematis. Pea pods and parsley complete the centrepiece, the parsley tucked discreetly amongst the vegetables to help keep them steady. Any vegetables and flowers in season – or out of season, if you're prepared to pay the price – are worth considering for a multiple display, and a single stem of flowers on each napkin adds a pretty, finishing touch.

introduced to Europe for the beauty of their crimson, sweet-pea-shaped flowers, and only later was their value as a vegetable discovered. They (like all members of the bean and pea family) are cousins of the ornamental sweet pea, and deserve to be considered as a source of flowers as well as food. Use them, the white flowers of garden peas, or the black-and-white flowers of broad beans, exactly as you would use sweet peas.

Alliums are much loved for their densely packed heads of star-like flowers which go a long way to disguising their secret: they are all ornamental members of the onion family. Equally pretty are the flowers of their edible cousins, garlic, chives, leeks (and onions themselves), but I would advise caution when using them as floral decoration indoors. I once picked masses of ransoms, the wild garlic that grows so profusely in damp English woodlands, and placed them carefully on the back seat of my car. The smell was soon unbearable and I learned my lesson.

GREEN AND PLEASANT

I will never be able to love unequivocally the formal garden. The would-be Versailles, whether tiny or immense, is not for me. In gardens it is informality that gives me the greatest pleasure. I love the *jardin anglais* which has no flowers, only grass, winding walks, long vistas, and, most importantly, trees. 'Capability' Brown was a master of this tradition, which has set the style for English country houses for more than two centuries. My other favourite is the country garden which has outgrown the limits set by any particular style. It should be full of roses, but without the coldly ordered formality of a rose garden; full of herbs, without intensely herbalist overtones, and full of other flowers, without a hint of academic classification.

FORM AND FOLIAGE

Besides their own inherent beauty, informal gardens are generous providers of the foliage we need for most of our arrangements. Leafy stems, twigs or branches (taken prudently and in moderation) are always available, with neither lasting nor temporary harm done. An informal garden is a flexible one and, once established, yields foliage for indoors without ever looking denuded. And the choice of foliage from your own garden is likely to be unique and personal to you, certainly unlike the limited, unimaginative supply that some florists have to offer.

Once you get your foliage indoors and conditioned (see pages 108–9), the respect with which you treat it and the attitude you take towards it are of paramount importance. All too often, foliage is looked upon as second-best, as a filler to eke out a few (usually expensive) flowers. I can look at an arrangement and tell at once if it was designed for a display of flowers but ended up with foliage used half-thoughtlessly, half-apologetically, without any awareness of its potential. Foliage can be the foundation but it can also be the sole component of a whole arrangement. No apologies are ever needed.

Look with fresh eyes at what foliage has to offer – its colour, form, shape, texture and scale – in exactly the same way that you evaluate flowers. And never underrate the colour green. It is a favourite of mine when I paint as well as when I make bouquets. I urge you to explore its many variations – the shiny, dark green of holly leaves, the incredibly fresh green of young beech leaves, the spiky, grey-green of pine foliage, the polished gleam of camellia leaves. I must also point out that the range of leaf colour goes far beyond green (and not just in autumn). Foliage offers a full palette – yellows, oranges, reds, pinks, greens, blue/greens, purples, browns, greys and white – for use when flowers are freely available as well as when they are scarce. Use foliage boldly, use it discreetly, but, above all, use it honestly.

VARIEGATED FOLIAGE

Foliage with built-in colour contrast is an instant problem solver. I would be lost without my variegated dogwoods. The silver-variegated leaves of *Cornus alba* 'Elegantissima' stay crisp and fresh looking for months. As I write, I can see mine through the window; the leaves are beginning to fall, revealing the bright crimson stems for winter arrangements. Another indispensable favourite is *Cornus alba* 'Spaethii', with bold, golden-yellow markings on its green leaves. Either of these, massed in a large but simple container, is strong enough to make an impression without the addition of a single flower.

The variegated sage, *Salvia officinalis* 'Tricolor', is one of my small-scale favourites. Its grey-green leaves are splashed with creamy white and suffused with crimson and pink. It definitely grows more slowly than dogwood, and sprigs rather than branches will have to suffice. Try it with pale pink roses. *Salvia officinalis* 'Icterina' is less showy – grey-green with splashes of yellow – but nonetheless I use it with the tiny yellow-green flowers of lady's mantle (*Alchemilla mollis*).

Fuchsia is known for its flowers but there is one, the hardy *Fuchsia magellanica* 'Versicolor' that I love for its foliage – a fuchsia with modest flowers but with elegant grey-green leaves and creamy-white markings, plus a crimson-pink glow particularly noticeable on young foliage.

There are so many common garden plants that come in variegated forms: holly, ivy, periwinkle, hosta, iris and privet, to name a few. It is a good idea to spend a Sunday afternoon at a good garden centre or botanical garden to see what is available and what catches your fancy. On the whole, variegated plants are slightly slower growing, sometimes smaller, than their wholly green-leaved cousins because variegated leaves contain less chlorophyll; nevertheless they are worth cultivating.

Certain leaves, while not strictly speaking variegated, do give double colour value for the space they take: the ones

Huge and perfectly simple Victorian glass battery jars contain an even more massive array of greenery. Sweet chestnut (with its spiny burrs), larch, pine, rhododendron, eucalyptus, berberis, cotinus and senecio together command the corner of a room. Flowers would be superfluous to this display, which captures the spontaneity and freshness of country woods and gardens.

Previous page
A wooden trug, lined and filled with leaves: ivy, both the plain form and the pale-centred 'Gold Heart'; hosta and thistle. (The green 'pompons' are newly formed ivy seed heads.) Leaves can be as richly varied in colour and form as flowers, and have the additional advantage of being more freely available, especially if you have a garden. If not, you'll still find foliage less expensive to buy than flowers, and even florists' foliage is worth looking at with a new eye.

that have a second, distinct colouring on the leaf underside. The glossy, bright green leaves of evergreen magnolia, *Magnolia grandiflora* 'Exmouth', have undersides of soft, suede-like texture, in deepest ruddy brown. When I grew up in America, a New York florist created a vogue for painting the soft undersides with white or pale pink matt paint for unexpected colour. The vogue has long since died out, but it might be worth reviving.

The white poplar *(Populus alba)* has woolly, white undersides to its dark green, maple-like leaves; the form 'Richardii' has bright yellow and woolly white leaves. It is a smaller tree, an advantage in many gardens. Silvery-white leaf undersides can be had from some of the rhododendrons, of which *Rhododendron grande* is probably the most remarkable. Its deep green shiny leaves can be 30cm (12in) or more in length, each with soft white 'felt' beneath. A single branch is impressive enough without any floral accompaniment; in fact, I can think of few flowers that can match its grandeur in size or scale. Another pink-tinged favourite of mine is the lovely balm of Gilead poplar *(Populus candicans* 'Aurora') whose young leaves are marbled with creamy white and pink, and bring with them, when used indoors, the lovely balsam scent.

You have an unexpected source of variegated leaves in your own collection of pot plants. Coleus, for example, with its striking colour combinations is not, I know, a universally admired plant (perhaps because of its Victorian overtones, and the fact that so many specimens are left to grow leafless and leggy). Try the combination of coleus leaves with bright autumn dahlias or chrysanthemums. Their colours match, and the effect is stunning. For a more subdued feel, fill a little basket with zonal geranium leaves, then put flowers between them, above and below, so that they seem to be peering out from the leaves. The variegated leaves help extend the flowers without depriving them of their beauty.

COLOUR CHOICE

I get my bright yellow foliage from several sources: a favourite is the golden-leaved philadelphus (*Philadelphus coronarius* 'Aureus'), whose flowers are insignificant compared to those of other philadelphus, but which has young foliage of a clear and clean yellow. Grown in shade, it has a slight lime-green tinge (not unattractive); grown in sun, the yellow is pure but the leaves can become scorched and disfigured. As the season progresses, the leaves take on a green overtone, so they are at their magical best in spring. The elder of hedgerows and woodlands has two sophisticated, yellow-leaved relations: the golden elder (*Sambucus nigra* 'Aurea'), and the golden cut-leaved elder (*Sambucus racemosa* 'Plumosa Aurea'). Both are tough and uncomplaining shrubs, although the cut-leaved form is slower growing and less generous in its foliage. At the other end of the scale, for tiny nosegays and other small but immaculate arrangements, try the clear yellow golden marjoram (*Origanum vulgare* 'Aureum'), or one of the many golden heathers: *Calluna vulgaris* 'Gold Haze' and *Erica carnea* 'Aurea' are good choices.

Purple foliage is marvellous but must be used with care. I have seen gardens where every possible leaf colour was present in close proximity, no doubt on the basis of 'the more, the merrier'. I have also encountered indoor displays of cut foliage where the deepest purple rubbed shoulders with the brightest yellow and jarring lime green, in a frenzied attempt to provide the proverbial blaze of colour. Don't. Each of these colours has such strong visual character that competition from other sources can result in an uncomfortable, even unpleasant, effect. My favourite purple comes from the smoke tree (*Cotinus coggygria* 'Royal Purple'). In summer, masses of pinky-mauve hairy inflorescences are produced, giving a hazy appearance to the bush, but it is the deep, wine-purple leaves that have earned it a place in my garden. Use it without flowers, if you can display it in front of a window or other light source; the leaves will appear translucent and quite breathtaking. In autumn, they take on a plum-red tone.

The purple beech (*Fagus sylvatica* 'Purpurea' and *Fagus sylvatica* 'Riversii') is a magnificent tree, and the avenues of purple beech occasionally seen in the English countryside are unforgettable. As with other beech foliage, the young leaves are inclined to wilt, and need a good long soak in water to keep them firm. The ornamental grape vine (*Vitis vinifera* 'Purpurea') produces reddish purple young leaves in spring, and in summer they take on rich bronzy-purple tones. Neither one has the pure colour of the purple beech foliage, but they are close enough to include here. Use them if you can in combination with their own purple grapes in autumn, or cheat with store-bought grapes earlier in the season.

The purple-leaved *Prunus cerasifera* 'Pissardii' is another standby. If left to its own devices it forms a small tree, but you can prune it into bush form for easier access. The young foliage is deep red, eventually becoming dark purple, usually appearing after the pale pink flowers.

The closest to blue you can achieve with leaves is provided by rue (*Ruta graveolens* 'Jackman's Blue'). The lacy – and it really is lacy – foliage helps cool down such 'hot' flowers as orange or red roses; try using it with rosehips in autumn. Rue has a slightly bitter smell, which some people find unpleasant. I agree that its own small, mustard-yellow flowers are not pretty and are best removed.

Not everyone's garden can accommodate the magnificent blue cedar (*Cedrus atlantica* 'Glauca') but if you can acquire a branch, one way or another, you'll find it extremely unusual. Its foliage is described as glaucous, which means that it has a waxy 'bloom' to it, an overtone of blue-grey or blue-white. Try it with pale pink flowers, or deep red.

After the blues come the greys and silvers. In my garden in Spain there are olive trees, some of which were planted when the Romans occupied the land. Later, when the Moors captured the area, additional trees were planted and now I have the luxury of their silvery leaves to enjoy indoors and in the garden. For more temperate climates, try the silver of the artemisia family. Two of my favourites are the herbaceous perennial *Artemisia absinthum* 'Lambrook Silver' and the shrub *Artemisia arborescens*. The leaves of the latter look like silver filigree and their presence adds elegance to any arrangement. The 'Lambrook Silver' form is named after the garden of the late Margery Fish, a well known English gardener and author, who loved their silky lacy leaves. Try them with old-fashioned garden pinks or roses, or with purple foliage for a sophisticated display.

Artemisias, like rue, have a strong aroma, and so does the foliage of eucalyptus, which I find unpleasant. I prefer to provide silver foliage from other sources. Still, if you don't mind its smell, eucalyptus is almost always readily available. The foliage is very long lasting and can pull its weight in several successive arrangements through the winter months (eventually becoming a good accompaniment to dried flowers). There are many species of varying degrees of hardness, but most have two forms of foliage: juvenile, which is the more sought after, and the less interesting, mature foliage. Try mixing eucalyptus with the scarlet-tinged winter foliage of *Mahonia japonica*. Eucalyptus which has been preserved in glycerine takes on a slightly purple tinge and sometimes the leaf veins alone turn purple in startling but pleasant contrast to the grey leaves.

Autumn provides a sudden (and all too short) wealth of leaf colours. This is more true in the United States than in England; perhaps most beautiful are the states of New England – Vermont, Maine, Massachusetts, Rhode Island, New Hampshire and Connecticut. The maples, above all, are the trees for autumn colour, and the sugar maple *(Acer saccharinum)* is queen of these. In England, its fiery shades

An autumnal arrangement, large scale and informal, that manages to include a bit of summer as well. Branches of beech, both fresh and glycerined, are combined with dried bracken; glycerined evergreen magnolia; yellow-tinged larch, and pink-tinged azalea leaves. The central focal point is the cluster of white antirrhinums. The real flowers would be almost impossible to come by, when autumn foliage is at its best, so a bit of judicious 'cheating', with silk flowers, is fully justified. Note the proportion of foliage to flower; the flowers sit like jewels in their leafy setting.

of orange, red and crimson are somewhat subdued (when compared to the display in America), but it is valuable even so. Birch, hornbeam and beech also provide autumn colour: the palest yellow birch, the deep rich brown of beech and hornbeam. The staghorn sumach *(Rhus typhina)* is another North American tree with brilliant autumn colour but the leaves are only good for a few hours of life — they wilt almost as soon as they are cut and no amount of conditioning prolongs their life. This is a problem to some degree with all autumn foliage, which only turns colour because it is starting to dehydrate and die in preparation for the plant's winter dormancy. The beauty that attracts us is inherently short-lived. I think this is even more reason to make the most of the few glorious weeks of autumn colour, even if it means replacing autumn foliage in an arrangement on a daily basis. Flowers such as dahlias, chrysanthemums, Japanese anemones, asters, sedums and goldenrods marry well with autumn leaves, as do the abundantly available berries and seed pods. Use them generously, as the Dutch painter Pieter Claesz did in one painting; a bouquet of leaves encircled by red berries.

Winter colours are, on the whole, longer lasting than the transitory colours of autumn. *Bergenia cordifolia*, commonly (and unfortunately) called 'pig squeak', has large, glossy, round leaves which become tinged with crimson and mahogany in winter. Among the conifers, Japanese cedar *(Cryptomeria japonica* 'Elegans') changes from blue-green to a deep russet red. Its foliage is quite unlike true cedars, being feathery and delicate, and it makes a lovely background for a few leafless sprigs of winter-flowering viburnum *(Viburnum fragrans,* now usually called *Viburnum farreri).* Some of the golden heathers take on scarlet winter hues: *Calluna vulgaris* 'Blazeaway' and *Erica cinerea* 'Golden Drop' are two. And some of the evergreen Kurume azaleas, notably 'Hino-crimson' and 'Stewart-sonian', have brilliant, wine-red winter foliage. They are so slow growing that a small sprig is all you can safely take at any one time. Use it with the care and precision of a jeweller to set off a small bunch of snowdrops or even a single winter-flowering iris.

GENERIC DELIGHTS

The genus *Hedera* (ivy, to all but the most botanically minded) is often a victim of misplaced snobbery. Because the common form. *Hedera helix,* grows wild and prolifically, it is looked upon almost as a weed and passed over when it comes to choosing plants to grow to use indoors. What a wasted opportunity! I admit that the Victorians went too far; they painstakingly trained it to grow along the mahogany frames of sofas, up the legs of pianos and even over fire screens (though how the heat-shy ivy fared once the screens were put to use is too grim a thought to dwell upon). Today, I use it in many ways: it is lovely with a lemon-laden table centrepiece, as shown on page 46, you could perhaps run long sprigs from the lemons to each place setting. Ivies can trail from containers or soften a stiff arrangement; they can wind up and disguise wooden dowels used to hold a high-rise ball of flowers for a table centrepiece. They can be made into a wreath surrounding a centrepiece of roses, or they can be used with their own berries in a simple wooden trug, with a few giant thistle leaves *(Onopordum acanthium)* for contrast and to fill any empty spaces (see page 52).

If common ivy is too plain for you, there are dozens of cultivars, each with a special colour or colour combination, shape and size. The large-leaved forms include the Persian ivies, most notably *Hedera colchica* 'Dentata Variegata' and *Hedera colchica* 'Paddy's Pride'. The former has huge leaves bordered with creamy white and the latter has central splashes of yellow and pale green, edged with dark green. Persian ivy is sometimes called elephant's-ear ivy, and for good reason: the individual leaves can grow to a length of 30cm (12in). They make an impressive contribution to all-foliage or mixed arrangements. There is also the lovely 'Cristata', with ruffled and twisted leaf edges; the small and tidy arrowhead ivy 'Sagittifolia', with pointed, arrow-shaped leaves, and the bright yellow 'Buttercup'. Some are splashed or edged in gold, silver, creamy grey or white, and there are the ones that turn a rich crimson red in winter. Use ivies to create a dark or brightly coloured setting for flowers, or use them as the star of the show.

Hostas – sometimes called funkias or plantain lilies – are an absolute necessity for me, outdoors and indoors. Their orderly and artistic habit of growth in the garden can easily be re-created inside in masses of cut foliage. Their own trumpet-shaped white or mauve flowers are not unattractive, but certainly of lesser value. Punctuate hosta foliage with cut flowers of your choice (I prefer white) and even make them peep out from beneath the leaves. Though there are many beautiful variegated and plain-leaved hostas, the one I prefer above all others is *Hosta sieboldiana* for its deeply veined, almost quilted, glaucous grey leaves. The bold veining is matched by its size; the leaves can grow to 60cm (24in) in length, and two or three of them can form an instant structure for a large bouquet. *Hosta undulata* is a much smaller plant altogether, with creamy-white leaves edged in green. The name 'undulata' comes from the way the leaves twist, spiral and, indeed, undulate. The Victorians were as maniacal about ferns as they were about ivies, and, like ivies, ferns fell into a long period of disrepute as a result. They are now back in favour again, though perhaps without quite the same zeal. The delicate lady fern *(Athyrium filix-femina)* and its larger and less frilly counterpart, the male fern *(Dryopteris filix-mas),* are lovely. Quite different in its appearance is the hart's tongue fern *(Phyllitis scolopendrium),* with its solid, glossy green fronds. Of the many bizarre forms of hart's-tongue fern collected and cherished by the Victorians, only the crested hart's tongue fern is seen today – and only rarely.

Florists are as much to blame for undervaluing ferns as the Victorians. They tend to pack the obligatory few fern fronds into the long-stemmed roses or mixed bouquets they prepare, just as an afterthought – and they look it. And nothing has a more 'store-bought' feel than this same lonely fern poking out of this same bouquet of flowers, unwrapped and placed in a room. It is far better to use no ferns at all, or to use them massively, as the bulk of the bouquet, enhanced with a few flowers.

Last, but certainly not least, come the spurges *(Euphorbia).* The poinsettia is a form of euphorbia, so is the crown of thorns, and so are a large number of desert cacti, but it is the garden euphorbia that contributes so much to flower and foliage arrangements. As with hostas, the flowers are incidental to the value of the foliage, though the small, yellow-green bracts of many forms are delightful. The deep green tidy leaf rosettes of *Euphorbia robbiae* look like flowers themselves, and can be used as such in all-foliage arrangements. *Euphorbia myrsinites* is intriguing rather than beautiful, with its lax trailing stems covered with pointed, glaucous foliage. A single stem, displayed in a small vase, looks as exotic as a spray of orchids, and few would guess its tough character and garden origins. Equally curious looking is the caper spurge *(Euphorbia lathyris),* which is reputed to keep moles at bay. I use its upright tall stems, which carry orderly sets of narrow, grey, horizontally held leaves, as architectural focal points in an arrangement. Though a typical English cottage-garden plant, there is something ultra-modern in its appearance. *Euphorbia characias* and its close relative *Euphorbia wolfenii* reach shrub-like proportions in the garden and provide stately, unbranched stems of blue-grey foliage.

All euphorbias exude a milky sap when cut (see page 109), which is a skin irritant and also poisonous, so handle them carefully and wash your hands immediately afterwards.

The glazed cachepot provides the flowers in this display; leaves alone suffice to fill it. Pittosporum, fern and the unusual *Raphiolepis umbellata* are arranged in rough layers, with sprigs of blue-grey rue and silver-green senecio tucked in as highlights. Note how the fern is used decisively and generously, not as a lost, last-minute afterthought.

CHEATING THE SEASONS

Like frozen peas, certain flowers – roses and chrysanthemums, for example – can be had all year round, month in and month out. While our Victorian ancestors would have been green with envy at the thought of our endless supply of these, as well as flowers from all over the globe, nevertheless certain months of the year are still difficult. In temperate zones, the late autumn, winter and early spring months are the relatively leafless and flowerless ones in the garden, and the expensive ones in the florists' shops. You can throw up your hands in despair, or you can take these months as a floral challenge. I, personally, prefer the latter and have spent years perfecting the art of cheating the seasons indoors: making summer last a little bit longer, making spring start a little bit earlier and extracting from the darkest autumn and winter days floral and foliage treasures. It isn't only a question of economy; lavish displays of expensive flowers can still be boring. I much prefer the modest but personalized bouquet of flowers, leaves and twigs that reflect the contents of my garden, nearby hedgerows or fields, at any single time of year. And if not fresh, then carefully and lovingly preserved, as a personal memento of past springs and summers. The more grey and lifeless my garden is (or the outdoor scene generally, when I am in the city) the more I try to create an indoor garden, and one that is as imaginative and unexpectedly original as possible.

POTTED PLANTS AND 'POT-ET-FLEUR'

Potted plants come into their own as a home's main winter garden, and no interior decorator worth his or her salt could consider a room finished without its quota of plants. They bring a different but equal beauty into the house and, in the cold months, they replace the elusive, out-of-season (and certainly more expensive) ones. If you think about it, cut flowers and foliage are dying (however slowly and discreetly) while potted plants go on living and displaying their beauty, some for years.

The potted plant is no less beautiful for all its durability. I've proven this with a collection of mixed plants grouped as a centrepiece on my table or using a single potted plant to dress up a dowdy corner – certainly to brighten a sick room. Remember, though, that the plants are living and long-term, inhospitable conditions should be avoided: no dark corners for sun-loving plants, no brightly lit window sills for shade-loving ferns, no draughty hallways and hot radiators. These are the most obvious mistakes, though most plants will come to no harm for a short period of time in less than ideal conditions. If you do want to leave a group of plants permanently in one spot, make sure they all like the same growing conditions and that these are roughly what you are providing.

The joy of using growing plants is their versatility. I often sow the seeds of three or four different plants in one large clay pot; when in bloom, they surprise you as a fascinating garden. You can also achieve the same effect by combining several grown plants in one big pot. They may look uneasy together to start with, but soon the plants will grow together and intermingle. Cyclamens, for example, seem too beautiful to pick (although if you do, the flowers are delightful and look like butterflies frozen in flight). Pots are better: place as many pots of cyclamen as possible in your largest basket. Use peat to fill the gaps between the pots and moss to cover all the surfaces so the flowers and their attractive leaves grow into a tiny, natural garden. I use gloxinias, wildly gypsy-coloured cinerarias, streptocarpus and azaleas in the same way. Though beautiful on their own, the beauty is multiplied by massing the pots together and you are also providing highly beneficial growing conditions. I have one simple square basket in which four pots fit perfectly, and it is in constant use.

Vegetables and fruit are unexpected additions to the potted-plant scene. Though flowerpots of tiny cherry tomatoes are taken for granted in the garden or green-house, they are unexpected and dramatic when placed in a row on a windowsill, or marching down a luncheon table or against wood panelling in a library or living-room. Decorative ornamental cabbages and kales are equally unusual house plants when placed on a low table, where you can look down on their extraordinary faces (some are in pinks and wines, some in yellow and greens). The fragrance of citrus flowers – oranges, lemons, limes and grapefruit – is overpoweringly lovely, and potted citrus plants, with their shiny fresh green foliage, provide beauty even when not in flower. They do need long, hot summers to ripen their wood enough to produce flowers and fruit. Still, if you have that descendant of the eighteenth-century orangeries, a conservatory or greenhouse, you may be able to provide the additional heat and light needed. Another unforgettable scent comes from hyacinths, which I like to group together for one strong accent, or place individually

Previous page
Definitely not for eating, these four small dishes, each filled with visually delectable treats, encapsulate the best of autumn. The bright green is provided by the prickly outer casings of sweet chestnuts. Blackberries, elderberries, viburnum berries and pink-berried sorbus, with sprigs of ivy and bracken, fill the adjacent dish. Assorted berries and rose hips, in various shades of red, combine with bright orange sea-buckthorn berries to encircle a central cushion of moss. In the leaf-edged dish (a mixture of elder and deciduous rhododendron leaves), nestle red berries and the curious, bright pink and orange berries of the spindle tree. Such a small scale, multiple arrangement is best seen at close range, so the delicate detail of the various 'ingredients' can be observed and admired.

Pot-et-fleur at its 'party best'. A Boston fern, with a chair for a plant stand, is dressed up with pink and white ranunculus. Flowers that wilt rapidly, such as these, should have their stems inserted in florists' vials first. Tougher flowers – chrysanthemums, for example – can have their stems inserted directly into the damp compost.

Pot-et-fleur works well on a less dramatic scale, too, with a small potted plant and two or three flowers.

around a room. Pots of scented-leafed geraniums lack the showy flowers of their more popular relatives, the zonal and regal geraniums, but the range of scents available, and their intensity, should be enough for any home. Some geranium leaves smell of peppermint, others of lemon, nutmeg and even rose.

Now roses: in the last few years the popularity of the miniature rose has increased beyond measure. All the beauty and fragrance of the rose was scaled down to a plant 30-45cm (12-18in) high, so that those with small gardens or no gardens at all could collect and grow roses. Though they are quite happy in window boxes, and in flowerpots in small courtyards and balconies, they are not really house plants. The low light levels, low humidity and high temperatures indoors simply do not suit them, and though you can display your miniature roses in pots for an evening party or even a special weekend, the sooner you return them to the garden or window box the healthier and more floriferous they will be.

This goes for bonsai plants too. Though often photographed in interior settings, they are definitely outdoor plants, to be enjoyed indoors for the briefest possible time. Even bay trees, which once graced the cold halls and sitting-rooms of Victorian homes, cannot stand up to the heated, indoor environment of today. Still, there is no reason not to enjoy them as short-term guests, either as they are or embellished with flowers or ribbons, as shown opposite. There are many other short-term guests from the garden that can decorate the indoors. Primroses, violets, lilies of the valley, snowdrops and even crocuses can be carefully dug up from the garden, with as much soil as possible clinging to the roots, and packed into flowerpots, shallow dishes and even large, transparent glasses with water. For the longest display and the least discomfort to the plants, keep them in a cool room; once the flowers fade, return the plants to the garden, where they should completely recover.

The bay trees shown here are a supreme example of what can be done extravagantly in the winter months to make the most of the florist's flowers. The technique of combining cut flowers with pot plants for a temporary display is called *pot-et-fleur*, and there is really very little in the way of technical knowledge needed. Armed with florists' vials and a bunch of small winter flowers – chrysanthemums and pinks are particularly suitable – you can transform foliage plants like the weeping fig *(Ficus benjamina)*, for example, into a floral display – though certainly not at a single stroke. Allow two or three hours, preferably with a friend

A pair of bay trees dressed up for Christmas. Dozens of bunches of small flowers and berries, tied with red or white satin ribbons, are tucked into the dark-green sprigs of bay. Gypsophila, carnations, freesias, chincherinchees, tiny 'button' chrysanthemums and pyracantha berries, all echoing the red and white colour scheme, are combined in mix-and-match fashion. This is definitely time-consuming, though eminently pleasant, to prepare, and two pairs of hands are better than one. Use transparent florists' vials for the flowers and spray regularly with a fine mist during preparation to keep the flowers fresh. It is a relatively short-term display, but you can change the shorter-lived flowers if they wilt.

helping, if you want a large-scale *pot-et-fleur*. Use ribbons for additional colour and to conceal the vials if necessary. Very thin wire is useful for fixing the flower-filled vials to the branches, though with densely branched plants the vials can simply be nestled in amongst the foliage. If you are using the nestling technique, then the plants must be in their final position before you start; there is nothing more frustrating than watching hours of work come unstuck as the plant is moved to its final position. If you are worried about littering the carpet with bits of twig and petals, spread out plastic or old sheeting before you start.

Though a large-scale *pot-et-fleur* is dramatically beautiful, there are many more occasions and budgets that call for a much smaller operation. A single maidenhair or Boston fern with a few rosebuds tucked in amongst the fronds may be botanically unlikely but will certainly be admired. So many begonia plants produce exquisite leaves – *Begonia boweri,* for example, with its velvety greeny-brown leaves, or many of the *Begonia rex* hybrids – which could, if you feel like it, be enhanced with a few, well-chosen cut flowers. Though not exactly *pot-et-fleur,* but still worth mentioning, is the practice of using growing plants, their roots cleaned of all soil or compost, with flowers in a water-filled container. Begonias are a prime example; the plants suffer no harm, and after adding colour and mass to a display, can be quietly potted in compost when the flowers die and the short-term show is over.

FORCING THE ISSUE

At the bleakest time of the year, you want to give nature a bit of a push. Though there is very little you can do with the weather outdoors, you can bring the garden – or part of it – indoors, and hurry it along into blossom. Forcing works particularly well with branches of some shrubs and trees such as forsythia, flowering almond, flowering quince, flowering currant and some flowering fruits (less well with others, but trial and error is again the best means ultimately to success). The most important guideline is to keep the shrub's or tree's welfare the first priority: some, like forsythia, grow quickly and replace branches cut for forcing by the end of the following summer, while others like witch hazel, beautiful and fragrant when forced indoors, take years to replace the branches that have provided short-term pleasure indoors in winter. Besides the growth rate, keep the shape of the plant in mind and try to combine the removal of branches for forcing with balancing the overall shape of the plant.

If cut in midwinter, it usually takes five or six weeks for

Branches of forced almond blossom need no adornment. Here they are displayed in a large woven basket, which conceals a bucket containing chicken wire and water. Once the branches are in position, pack the space between the bucket and the basket with sphagnum moss, peat, pebbles or even crumpled newspaper, then top with a layer of bun moss. Remember to mist the moss regularly, to keep it fresh and green.

A botanical pun (prunes and flowering almond are both members of the genus *Prunus*) which is a visual treat for botanists and non-botanists alike. The flower stalks are too short to be inserted into florists' vials, so remove the flowers from the branches at the last possible moment and tuck them gently into the mounded prunes. Present the display at the end of a winter or early spring dinner party, for a pretty and memorable finale.

dormant branches to flower (or produce catkins). It seems like much too long a time to wait, but I assure you they will still be far in advance of those out of doors. Smash 5-7.5cm (2-3in) of the cut end of the stem, and give the material a long, deep drink of warm water. The first day or two, keep the branches in their water-filled bucket in a cold (but not frosty) spot, then move them into the warmth. Change the water regularly, and spray the branches with a fine mist of warm water from time to time to encourage the branch to become active and produce its spring growth. The warmer it was outdoors when you cut the branches and the closer to the plant's natural display period, the quicker the forcing process will be. On the other hand, they will seem less exotic and precious if the garden is nearly in flower and winter all but over.

Forcing tends to take the colour intensity from a flower and replace it with a paler tone. While this doesn't matter with white flowers, you may want the deep crimson rose of a flowering currant instead of the palest pink. If this is the case, you can retain at least some of the rich colour by exposing the opening blossom to bright sunshine. If you want a mixture of colours, keep some in the shade, others in a sunny spot.

If you are lucky enough to have an orchard or any fruit trees, you have a ready-made source for forcing flowers. Plum and apple, cherry, pear, peach and apricot are all worth forcing, and if the branches are covered with bits of greeny-grey lichen, so much the better. Try their ornamental equivalents too: the flowering crabs, cherries, quinces. And don't forget forcing foliage. Watching the huge sticky buds of horse chestnut unfurl into fresh green, many-fingered leaves is as exciting to me as watching a rose-bud open, and really does convey a feeling of spring. Try forcing beech and hornbeam, the delicate Japanese maple and its common garden cousin, sycamore. The latter, though scorned as a dull, uninteresting tree, produces young foliage of delicate beauty, fresh green but tinged with rose red. Whitebeam *(Sorbus aria)* is at its most beautiful when coming into bud. The unfolding leaves really do look white, and because they are carried pointing upwards, the overall effect, with the pale leaf buds and dark stems, is like that of a candelabra. From a distance, the white unfolding leaves look like magnolias, too; use the branches with as much respect as you would give to a branch of magnolia in flower.

Besides the popular catkins of pussy willow, try forcing winter branches of alder. The angular habit of growth is starkly oriental and quite stunning in its leafless simplicity.

Watch the male and female catkins unfurl in the warmth indoors. Other delights can be had from winter-flowering plants brought on indoors. Winter-flowering jasmine *(Jasminum nudiflorum)* is probably the best known – but far too often taken for granted simply because it is so obliging and uncomplaining. You can cut the green branches in bud and bring them indoors to enjoy their delicate, papery-thin flowers in close up – left out in the cold they often do not get the attention they deserve.

As well as forcing branches into blossom or leaf, entire plants can be treated in the same way. You can force container-grown roses, lilac, viburnum and deutzias into

A shallow terracotta dish, normally used under a flower pot, makes a home for an indoor bulb garden. Lilac, yellow and deep purple crocuses, snowdrops and yellow miniature iris will live happily for a week or so packed in damp peat or compost covered with moss. When flowering is over, they can then be returned to the garden, to recover and flower again in following years. Here lichen collected from tree trunks adds a cool grey note to the brightly coloured flowers. Save it for re-use in later displays.

early flowering by moving them into a heated greenhouse in midwinter and then transferring them indoors for their final display. But if you don't have a heated greenhouse, forcing specially treated flower bulbs – hyacinths, tulips, daffodils and narcissi – is a much more realistic pursuit. With all these bulbs, it is important to keep them in a cool (but frost free) dark place until the pale green shoots are visible. Gradually move them into warmer and lighter conditions; the pale green will become darker and the flower bud will develop to its full potential. More of these lovely bulbs are killed by the mistaken kindness of bringing them into the warmth prematurely than by anything else.

FRUITFUL THOUGHTS

As the spring and summer seasons progress, flowers fade and are followed by ripening seed, often encased in berries or fruit, which are a source of great delight in the garden. I admit that ornamental fruit can never totally replace flowers indoors, but I ardently suggest you give them the respect and imagination they deserve. I cannot say enough for the ornamental crab apple tree in front of our house, and the two recommended are *Malus* 'John Downie' and 'Golden Hornet'. The first, with its miniature, red-tinged apples, and the second, with its golden-yellow ones, provide as much colour as any flower and also the additional joy of fruitfulness. Strip the quite ordinary leaves (they would wilt anyway) to display just the fruit and darkly attractive branches which complement perfectly the late autumn flowers, such as those shown on page 114, in both large and small-scale displays. Don't be deceived by their ornamental status; I save any fruits that I snip off or which fall off in the course of arrangement for making delicious jellies, or I cook them briefly to serve around roast pork for a culinary treat.

Black is a hard enough colour to find in the flower world (the nearly black tulip, for example is much admired and almost revered). Black berries are easier to find, and worth using extravagantly. Besides the aptly named blackberry – not necessarily those growing wild in the hedgerows but in several cultivated forms – there are the rich, wine black elderberries. They are even deeper in colour than the deepest rose or dahlia, with which I use elderberries to intensify already rich colours. One caution: elderberry makes a sumptuous but hazardous decoration because the berries tend to drop off at the slightest disturbance. Beware! Their staining power is incredible. Treat them with care and respect and check constantly for berries falling onto your carpets. Their own drab foliage is best removed. I sometimes make an arrangement with blackberries and elderberries forming a delicate 'hem' for a tightly packed display of roses and chrysanthemums. Privet, that much maligned hedging plant, produces fine pyramids of shiny black berries in autumn; ivy, in its mature form, has pretty heads of green berries (see page 52) that turn black in time for Christmas. The clustered berries of mahonia shade towards blue-black – looking like miniature grapes. Like grapes, they give a feeling of abundance to your efforts, so use them for contrast, to spike bunches of pale flowers, or to intensify leaf colours.

In the flower world, pure white is as stunning as black, and this is true of berries as well. The undistinguished snowberry bush *(Symphoricarpos)* has an untidy growth habit, very ordinary leaves and insignificant flowers. However, from early autumn onwards it more than earns its keep by producing densely packed clusters of large berries. Strip the leaves and use the white berries with white roses or to contrast with the deep reds and browns of autumn foliage. Though *Sorbus* (whitebeam and rowan are both members of this genus) is better known for its orange berries, there are also some stunning, pale-berried forms. Those of *Sorbus* 'Joseph Rock' are creamy yellow, while *Sorbus hupehensis* produces beautiful pink-tinged white clusters. Creamy-yellow berries can be had from firethorns (be very careful of the perniciously long thorns and snip them off with secateurs before using). Cotoneasters provide masses of red berries, and so do the hollies.

I love green berries as much as green leaves and even the rare green flower. Try the bright green, unripe berries of holly or aucuba (without their leaves for the best effect) with late summer flowers. The prickly green casings of sweet chestnuts add a particularly fresh colour. This green, from a most unexpected source, is lovely with pink, mauve or white flowers. Experiment by using it with bright yellow, green-eyed chrysanthemums as well; the green of the chestnut is strong enough to hold its own.

Because the vast majority of berries are in the orange and red family (so coloured to attract birds and thus ensure the wide dispersal of the plant's seeds) I have left them till last, although I would never undervalue them as they do give enormous pleasure at a rather dreary time of the year. Once Beverley Nichols and I were in his garden at the very end of the season. Where he previously had hundreds of flowers from which to choose, he now had to make very difficult choices. Starting with the three roses remaining in bloom, he added a few not-yet-frost-bitten stocks, a dandelion from a sheltered hedgerow, a wallflower, a marigold, a few late pansies, a sprig of Michaelmas daisy and masses of red berries. He put all these often-spurned odds and ends together in a large, brightly painted Italian marmalade pot. With the few flowers and many red berries he picked, he made an exciting point of not being beaten by scarcity.

After the last of the berries, then what? You can get your colour from ornamental barks: dogwoods *(Cornus)* are perhaps most well known for this. *Cornus alba* 'Elegantissima' has fiery red stems, brilliant against a white brick wall, and *Cornus stolonifera* 'Flaviramea' has bright yellow stems, strong enough visually to be the sole occupant of a large container provided the stems are generously massed.

Even one or two twigs will bring winter cheer to a cup and saucer, for example, filled with miniature ivy and moss. There are willows that produce young stems of a lovely purple hue, as well as red-stemmed and yellow-stemmed varieties. These, I'm afraid, are not seen in florists' shops; you'll have to rely on your own garden, or that of a friend, or lovely woodland walks for your supplies.

With some leafless branches, form is everything. Neither the alder nor the corkscrew hazel (*Corylus avellana* 'Contorta') has colour worth mentioning, but their habit of growth is starkly impressive and, again, a large glass container filled with massed branches of either sort provides beauty equal to any floral display. Emphasize their size and scale by putting arrangements at floor level, where they will seem like a miniature winter woodland brought indoors. Incidentally, I've found that a certain amount of artful improvement can take place beforehand: if the branches are of young wood, wet them, as basket makers do; the branches then become pliable enough to bend into a more pleasing shape, which can be fixed with fine wire and left to dry. This is a case of wire aiding art – a means to an end and certainly not an end in itself. Remove the wire once its work is done.

Fake flowers again, this time with the balance between the real and artificial reversed. Long-stemmed, white tulips, with their frankly fake leaves, share a pair of octagonal vases with sprigs of (real) Mexican orange blossom. The setting – a 'thirties drinks trolley – emphasizes the period flavour of the display, based unashamedly on the artificial.

FABULOUS FAKES

The artificial flower has come of age again, after many years of understandable disfavour. The Victorians, ever inventive, created flowers out of beads, feathers, shells, wax, fabrics and any other material that was at hand. The finished products, though technically remarkable, lacked the fresh feeling of a living flower; protected from dust inside glass domes, their lifelessness was emphasized. Their own fussy construction and appearance symbolized the fussiness of Victorian rooms.

Today's equivalents are now at the height of fashion. Though some artificial flowers are relatively expensive to buy, they are long-term bargains because they only 'die' when dust, dirt and a considerable passage of time have 'wilted' them. The standard of the silk and silk-like flowers (produced largely in the Far East) is now absolutely first class. Chrysanthemums, violets, tulips, lilies, gerberas and paeonies really do mimic their living models – with the same subtle colour gradation, variations from flower to flower and even petal to petal. Such artificial silk flowers are now socially classless – found in castles and cottages and everywhere in between. They can also remove seasonal restrictions which still exist despite modern technology and air transport. It is still impossible in most places, for instance, to get tulips or daffodils in summer or fall. Silk ones come to the rescue.

Lack of time, lack of money, lack of garden and lack of patience, or any combination thereof, are reasons to give artificial flowers a try. Silk flowers may be the most agreeable, but paper, straw, feather, bead and wax flowers are

also worth trying. Plastic? *Never.* And keep away from the inexpensive polyester flowers that have fiercely chemical colours, rather like a badly tuned colour television. Some blatantly artificial flowers can be exquisite; many polyester flowers certainly aren't. It is far safer, and a better investment, to buy fewer of the higher quality.

Use artificial flowers with the same care, love and imagination you would give living flowers. Put aside any thought of a tightly formal, rigid arrangement shaped like an asymmetrical triangle, pyramid, oval or crescent. The combination of artificial flower and artificial posturing is a terrible one and somehow, the more flowers you add the worse it gets. Instead, try a small bouquet of silk violets tucked into a few fresh leaves, or put three dozen silk daffodils into a copper basin, with sprigs of ivy or evergreen honeysuckle tucked in. I have several tiny baskets, moss covered, some with artificial miniature silk roses and others with miniature silk anemones (all tightly packed) – both are equal to their real counterparts in charm and beauty. Any one of these would be charming and cheerful all year as well as in cold winter months.

One of the keys to using artificial flowers well is to mix them with the real thing. Artificial flowers with living foliage, artificial foliage with living flowers, either of them with dried flowers; the combinations and possibilities are endless. A few which have made a deep impression on my mind, and which you might like to try, include fresh pink geraniums with dark red silk chrysanthemums, orange silk poppies with turning autumn leaves, and a crystal bowl packed with real fern and punctuated by a few small white silk roses. On page 59 I have used silk antirrhinums to spike autumn foliage, and you could use white silk roses to the same effect. When you're combining artificial and living material, daring, almost unthinkable, experiments with colour can be very rewarding: pink or deep red garnet roses with silk violets, for example, or real pink tulips, massed head to head with silk tulips in mixed colours.

DRIED AND PRESERVED FLOWERS

Sadly, dried flowers often bring to mind layers of dust, faded beauty and only the weakest remembrance of the original fresh flowers they once were. This is probably because of the insensitive way they are selected, arranged initially and cared for afterwards. The same old, tired, predictable bulrushes, yarrow, hydrangeas and statice are bought, haphazardly jammed into a container and left to the elements indoors. Dust settles, sunlight fades colours even further, and occasionally breakages occur. Because they are well and truly dead, there is no change and development to watch: no buds opening to reveal wide-faced flowers, no seed heads forming, no wilting or deepening colours. And while we regularly care for – even fuss over – cut fresh flowers, making minor adjustments such as new additions (and a few subtractions) from day to day, dried arrangements can – and often do – go for years without attention, dusty and unloved.

These same dried flowers can be the material of a high art form, given a change of attitude. In London, Kenneth Turner has done just that, and has carried his magnificent matchless art to the other side of the Atlantic. His highly original and fantastic arrangements are much sought after. I recently asked his help in sorting out a dark, awkward corner of my London drawing-room. His solution was a huge, truly wondrous bouquet of dried flowers in every shade of pink and wine, which looked beautiful against Wedgwood blue walls. Its sheer mass and scale make an unforgettable sight. If you have the time, inclination and enough dried flowers, you can repeat his success at a fraction of its price. Start with a central framework of chicken wire around a core of dry plastic foam. It may take days to cover it all over with flowers, but there is no hurry – nothing will wilt – and the result will be glorious.

New ways with dried flowers are the 'in' thing at the moment. The material itself is available in a huge range of species, sizes and colours, and includes dried grasses, seed pods and berries as well as dried flowers. Florists, larger department stores and stores specializing in 'country crafts' carry dried flowers, and stock them in such variety that choosing only a limited number can be a difficult task. Therefore, drying your own flowers, like making your own pot-pourri, is largely unnecessary. But do it; I find that it is such unnecessary tasks, done voluntarily, that give great pleasure and reveal your own personality when done. Knitting your own sweaters and baking your own bread are similar pleasurable activities.

The most natural and best time of the year to dry flowers is in the hot summer months. One July day in London I went to Pulbrook & Gould, the London florist which is so beautiful that is has become a tourist attraction. There, in the open workroom behind the shop, rows and rows of roses were hanging upside down on wires to dry. Many of the flowers are supplied from the gardens of Lady Pulbrook's friends and the whole effect was that of a magical garden turned upside down.

There are five basic methods of drying flowers and foliage, depending on the nature of the plant material and the effect you want to achieve. Needless to say, select perfect or near-perfect flowers and leaves, whichever method you choose. Flowers that have not yet reached the peak of their beauty are better subjects than those in full bloom when picked. Picking material for drying on a wet day is counter-productive, so wait until the weather has cleared up.

Hang-ups: air-drying by hanging flowers and foliage upside down in a warm, dry, dark place is a good method to begin with. Virtually all those of the everlasting varieties – helichrysum, yarrow, pearl everlasting, statice, helipterum and sea holly – should be air dried, as should various thistles (including globe artichokes), lavender, larkspur, love-lies-bleeding, delphiniums and acanthus. Seed heads and pods are also prime candidates for this method. Besides the well known honesty, bulrush, Chinese lantern and pampas grass, try hanging big seed heads of cow parsley (Queen Anne's lace), hollyhocks, allium, oriental poppies and love-in-a-mist upside down to dry. Strip the leaves off before hanging the seed heads up, singly if they are delicate, or in small bunches, so that the air can circulate freely around the flowers or pods. A warm, dark, dry, airy room is necessary. It is hard to go wrong if you choose a suitable place. If you are using a shed or garage, make sure it isn't damp, a not uncommon problem in British summers. An airing cupboard used by the British is a good solution if only for a few flowers at a time; if it is crowded with dehydrating flowers, the moisture that builds up has nowhere to go. You can run clothes lines or wire across the pantry ceiling and hang the upside-down bunches from it, but be careful to leave space for air to circulate freely. Remember that the faster the drying takes place, the more successful the exercise will be, and the more the original colour is retained. Leave the flowers, pods or seed heads until they are papery dry; in warm weather and with thin-petalled specimens, the process could be complete in a week; in damp weather and with thick-petalled subjects, it could take three weeks or more. Check them from time to time; the stalks tend to shrink as the moisture leaves them, and some could slip out from the tight bunches.

Wet and dry: it seems counterproductive to dry some flowers by putting them in water, but I promise you that it works. Hydrangeas are prime candidates, and so are hosta seed heads, heather, proteus and bells of Ireland. Wait until the flowers have started to dry and go papery on the stems before you pick them. Strip the leaves if practicable (heather is the exception), then put the flowers, right way up, in a container with 1cm ($\frac{1}{2}$in) water. Then, to retain the rich colour, keep them in a dark, airy place. The warmer the temperature (within reason), the quicker they'll dry; the process should be complete by the time the water in the container has evaporated.

Desiccation: this is the one method with an air of mystery, even magic, about it, but quite wrongly so. What happens is that the desiccant used – silica gel, alum, borax or hot

A dried flower 'high-rise', based on a mixture of wild grasses and garden flowers. The 'moss' at the base of the arrangement is dried hornbeam flowers, a more unusual and certainly less expensive alternative to dried reindeer moss.

To make this floral tree, shape plastic foam into a rough ball, cover it with chicken wire, then firmly secure it onto a thin wooden dowel. Next, 'plant' the dowel in a flower pot or other suitable container, filled and anchored with pebbles.

Before starting to fix the flowers in position, decide where the tree is to go, and whether it will be viewed from one side or from all round. If viewed from one side only, you can mass your 'best' flowers and grasses accordingly.

sand – draws out every bit of moisture from the petals, leaving the flower intact and with much of the original natural shape and colour retained. Silica gel is the best and quickest desiccant but, sadly, the most expensive. Still, you can re-use it almost indefinitely by drying it out after each use in a very low oven, which I find justifies the extra expense. The flowers to use are a matter of personal choice, but all of the following are suitable: roses, dahlias, zinnias, marigolds, carnations, pinks, daffodils, pansies, clematis, iris, hellebores, tulips, poppies and cosmos. Try others: the worst that can happen is the loss of a flower that would have eventually died anyway.

How to do it? Fill an airtight box with a 2.5cm (1 in) layer of desiccant, then place the flowers on top. Most are best done face upwards, but zinnias, for some reason, work best face downwards, and flowers with long stalks – delphiniums or bells or Ireland, for example – are laid lengthways on the desiccant. A dress box is the best container for such large-scale subjects. Next, very slowly and carefully sift the desiccant over the flower, so that it is gradually and totally surrounded by grains. If you leave any air pockets the weight of the desiccant will crush the petals as it settles. Also, the petals not in contact with desiccant will retain their own moisture and eventually rot. It is a delicate and exacting procedure. You many find a small paintbrush or skewer helpful in directing the grains into every crevice. Slowly build up a layer 2.5cm (1 in) thick above the flower (or flowers), then put a lid tightly on the container and leave in warm dry conditions for 3 – 4 days if you are using silica gel, a week if using any of the other desiccants. At the end of the time, carefully reverse the process, very gently sifting the grains away from the flower until you can gradually tip it out. The flower which isn't quite dry should be reburied and left for two or three days (not too long, though, or the flowers will be brittle and papery thin and will crumble at the slightest touch).

I like to display these flowers as faces to look into, but if you want to use them more traditionally, attach wire to the remaining stalk stub.

Pressing matters: our forebears were fond of pressing flowers to make into pictures, and the late Princess Grace of Monaco spent many hours creating paintings of pressed flowers in a small room set aside in the royal palace. She used weights of every size and type, often large catalogues, to press and preserve the prepared flowers. Hers was a lavish set-up that is not really necessary. A few sheets of blotting paper, telephone directories or a small, commercially available flower press will give good results. Flowers

Freshly picked roses being prepared for drying in a borax desiccant. Gradually, the level of the desiccant is built up so that the flowers are totally and completely buried.

with thin petals and clear, bright colours are best; those with thick, fleshy petals are unsuitable and those with subtle colouring tend to end up looking dull.

Pick the flowers on a dry day and in peak condition. Press the flower heads, without their stems and leaves; if you want these, press them separately. Many-petalled flowers – roses and double chrysanthemums, for example – are best dismantled and pressed individually as single petals, to be reconstructed on the 'canvas' later. Start by placing the flowers or petals in a single layer between sheets of clean, white blotting paper in a press (it can be a phone directory or heavy book). Make a note of what's inside, and forget about them for at least two months. The longer they are left (six months is ideal) the less quickly they will fade. Brilliantly coloured autumn leaves and silvery-grey leaves are lovely pressed this way.

Whole branches of leaves (beech is the traditional material), large fern and bracken (for three-dimensional displays rather than two-dimensional pictures) require a slightly different technique. Spread them out in a single layer between thick sections of newspaper and put the whole lot under the carpet in a seldom-used room. If that is not possible, put them under a small carpet under the couch. Leave for a month before using. As with air dried material, pressed material is very brittle and fragile, and cannot be coerced into any shape other than the one it had when placed under pressure. Use them as part of a mixed display of fresh flowers and foliage, or the more natural-looking glycerined material, to conceal any rigidity.

Glycerine is more often used to preserve foliage than flowers, and is used mixed with water – in the proportion of I part glycerine to 2 parts hot water. Colours, rather than fading as in the case of air drying, become a rich, bronzy brown in many cases, a pale biscuit or straw colour in others. Glycerine is expensive, so to make the most of it use tall, narrow containers, filled with 15cm (6in) of the glycerine-and-water mixture. Woody stems – those of mahonia, camellia, magnolia, laurel, cotoneaster, Mexican orange *(Choisya ternata)*, box and eleagnus, for example – will need hammering first so they can absorb the mixture freely. Non-woody foliage that benefit from the glycerine treatment include ferns, aspidistra leaves, hellebore leaves, bergenia leaves and the lovely, arching Solomon's seal *(Polygonatum)*. Some people use the mixture to preserve pussy willow catkins, clematis seed-heads, rose hips, iris seed pods and cotoneaster berries. Since the glycerine will be absorbed by the stems it is not necessary for the complete plant to be immersed in the mixture.

How long you leave the material in the glycerine varies; you can sometimes chart the progress of the glycerine as it moves up the stem by the colour change in the leaves. Thin leaves, such as those of beech and sweet chestnut, may take only a week, while thicker, evergreen leaves, such as fatsia and eleagnus, may need six weeks to become completely preserved. If you wish to preserve *individual* leaves it is standard practice to submerge them totally in the glycerine and water mixture. Leaves of mahonia, bergenia, ivy, fatsia and rhododendron respond to this treatment.

There is one great advantage of using the glycerine method: the leaves retain their natural shape and flexibility. Unlike air drying, which results in fragile, brittle and largely poker-straight material, glycerine-treated foliage looks glossy, bronzed and natural — not awkward versions of their former selves.

Don't forget to fill the container with more glycerine and water as the original lot gets absorbed. A less important procedure, but still useful, is to dab the leaves gently, top and underside, with the same mixture, to keep them from curling before they have fully absorbed the glycerine through the stems. A word of advice: very young, immature leaves don't take glycerine well, nor do leaves that have started to turn colour in autumn. Because glycerine is so expensive, I advise you to inspect each branch for imperfect leaves and remove them before placing the branch in the mixture.

ARTISTRY AND AFTERCARE

Preserving flowers and foliage requires a purely technical skill, and, without doubt, an admirable one — but using what you've preserved is an art. They need the same creative thought you would give fresh flowers, beginning with the container: remember that it will probably be visible for a long, long time. Still, never treat the preserved arrangement as a *fait accompli*; add to it, take away from it, rearrange its contents — and most excitingly pep it up with fresh flowers and foliage inserted with their own supply of water in individual florist's vials. Never put dried material in a water-filled arrangement unless you are prepared to lose it; once wet, it soon rots. Some fresh flowers — the most suitable are hydrangeas, mimosa, heather, yarrow and the lovely South African proteas — can be added at any time to dried arrangements, where they, too, will eventually dry out themselves. Not all flowers will respond well to this treatment: many dry out from the neck first, causing the flower head to hang and wilt in a desolate way. Try a few to start with and, if successful, add more. The

A huge and tightly packed bunch of lavender forms the central focal point and adds verticality to this lavish display of dried flowers. Though seemingly randomly arranged, the two-tier system — mixed flowers beneath and lavender on top — keeps the display from being chaotic. Unless you grow and dry the flowers yourself, dried flowers on this scale are undoubtedly expensive, but they will last and give pleasure for years. You can re-arrange them, add more or throw away the oldest and most faded, so you need never become bored with a particular display, and the initial investment should pay for itself many times over.

point is this: a static arrangement is virtually an abandoned one, and very quickly shows it. In the course of a winter, I gradually change the entire contents and nature of a dried arrangement as new flowers or foliage become available (and existing material becomes dusty or simply looks boring). To me, dried arrangements are three-dimensional paintings, to be gradually developed and improved, from the first sketchy impression to the fully finished and as-near-perfect-as-possible final image.

I mix dried viburnum berries with dried ferns, autumn leaves, trailing vines and such tawny yellow fruit as quince, kumquat and yellow tomato – not terribly long lasting, I admit, but memorable. Try dried vine leaves with dark grapes, punctuated by a single pink rose. Some of the ornamental vines – *Vitis vinifera* 'Brandt', 'Purpurea' or the brilliant crimson *Vitis coignetiae*, for example – are much more accessible and equally effective. I fill the largest crock I have with dried gypsophila and insert a changing display of a few fresh flowers (each inside its own florists' vial). Use the long-stemmed, beautifully curving bells of Ireland with erect bulrushes for tall arrangements; the lettuce green of the former sets off the latter to perfection, while the contrast in forms is stunning.

I use bird feathers (nag the poulterer for pheasant feathers or the not-quite-so-beautiful goose feathers) to decorate autumn foliage and flowers. The feathers last forever; they can also be used flat, to form a circle radiating from a central display or inserted carefully to 'spike' a flower arrangement. Unconventional, perhaps, but eye-catching and imaginative, and that's what counts.

POT-POURRI

At the time of the Great Plague, mixtures of rose petals, rosemary, juniper, bay leaves and frankincense were burned in chafing dishes (the word perfume is derived from Latin and means 'through smoke') and carried from room to room, in a futile attempt to ward off the disease. Such essential animal oils as musk from musk deer, civet from the wild cat and ambergris from the whale were generously used to augment the strength of scent from flowers and herbs. There were entire rooms, called stillrooms, set aside for the preparation of such fragrant mixtures, which were considered as much medical and pharmaceutical necessities as pleasurable additions to the domestic scene. They also had the awesome job of overcoming far from pleasant smells, in unventilated, musty rooms.

By the nineteenth century, improved hygiene, sanitation and medical knowledge made heavy and permanently present scents unnecessary. Victorian women preferred softer shadings of perfume, and relied less on the strong, animal oils for their pot-pourris; roses, mignonette, heliotrope, acacia, lavender, balm, basil, clover and bay leaves were their standbys, kept in tightly covered jars which were opened to sweeten the air whenever guests used the room (the lid was quickly replaced once the room was empty). Today, thousands like me use the fresh fragrance of pot-pourri in guest rooms as a symbol of hospitality.

A selection of pot-pourris. The traditional (and my favourite) rose pot-pourri in the centre is flanked by (clockwise from the lower left) lavender pot-pourri, a mixed pot-pourri based on marigold petals, a cottage garden mixture, and a lemon verbena leaf and violet mixture. Keep pot-pourris covered when they are not in use, to prolong their delicious fragrance.

Commercially produced pot-pourris are extremely popular, and are no longer found only at exclusive, expensive shops. A wide range of good quality pot-pourris is available from most large department stores, many gift stores, florists and even chemists. Still, there is a special pride and pleasure to be had from making your own: it may

be a complicated process but it is enjoyable, more economical and more personal than ready-made mixtures. Some of my favourite 'recipes' are given below, but please don't follow them exactly; treat them as a source of ideas – springboards for your own creativity.

Rose petals form the major ingredient (in fact, the only floral ingredient in some) because they retain their fragrance longer than most other flowers. I am a confirmed rose lover, but remember that not all roses are equally scented, so choose yours with this in mind. Try to find the old-fashioned, heavily scented moss, damask and rugosa roses or many of the modern, large-flowered (hybrid tea) roses. Lavender is probably best known for its lingering fragrance and, as with roses, there are pot-pourris composed entirely of its dried blossom. Other fragrant flowers to grow (or buy) for making pot-pourri include heliotrope, the old-fashioned sweet peas (if they are fragrant), old-fashioned pinks, sweet violet *(Viola odorata, Viola blanda)*, jasmine, lilac, marigold, lily-of-the-valley, mignonette, night-scented stock and valerian *(Centranthus ruber, Valeriana officinalis)*. Sources of aromatic leaves include the amazingly strong lemon verbena and others like sweet basil, rosemary, all the various mints, rose and other scented geraniums, thyme, myrtle, chamomile, tansy *(Chrysanthemum corymbosum)*, lavender cotton *(Santolina chamaecyparissus)* and hyssop.

Spices have no bulk or visual charm, but they are essential for boosting and enhancing the fragrance from the petals and leaves. The most common spices used in pot-pourris include cloves, cinnamon, allspice and nutmeg. The peel of citrus fruit – oranges, lemons and limes – with its clean, sharp fragrance, is sometimes called for in old-fashioned pot-pourris to add to the intense fragrance of the various flowers themselves.

Another bodiless source of fragrance are the essential oils. These sometimes play a supporting role to dried flowers already in the mixture: oil of roses, oil of lavender, violet, rose geranium, lemon verbena, or rosemary. Or one can add such enhancing scents as sandalwood or cedarwood. The secret is to use them with discretion; one drop too many can spoil an entire mixture (adding too little is far better than adding too much). They can be bought in fragrance shops. (I use bath oils myself.)

Traditionally, musk, civet and ambergris were favoured as fixatives – ingredients which absorbed and held, or 'fixed', the volatile and quickly disappearing scents of the flowers and herbs themselves. Nowadays, orrisroot *(Iris florentina)* performs the same task.

There are two basic ways to treat the ingredients for pot-pourri: preserve them dry or make a wet, or moist, mixture – which is the more historically 'correct'. The word pot-pourri is derived from French, meaning 'rotten pot'. This involves packing partially dried petals in layers of salt until they decompose and ferment to form a solid, cake-like mass which is then crumbled and mixed with essential oils, fixatives and dried petals. It is certainly the less visually attractive method, but is said to have a longer-lasting fragrance. For me, how a pot-pourri looks is just as important as how it smells, so I prefer the fully dried method – and dry really does mean bone dry. Pick whatever flowers you are using in the morning after the dew has dried but before the sun has risen to its full height. Spread the petals in a single layer on newspaper or, preferably, a fine window screen (more easily available in America than in Britain), and put in a dark, warm, airy and, above all, dry, spot. Never attempt to dry flowers in direct sunlight, or their colours will fade; and make sure that the air circulates freely around the flowers. Leave them to dry (it can take two days or two weeks – only watching will tell) until the petals have a crisp, dry texture.

Use the same treatment for herbs or fragrant leaves, though you can save time by hanging entire sprigs, in bunches, upside down to dry in warm, dry conditions, then stripping off the leaves two weeks later. Using a clothes line indoors in a warm, dry room or even outside during a long fine spell is a good idea.

The choice of ingredients and the proportions of each are up to you; the scents you prefer and what you have available will be the determining factors. However, here is a basic recipe, easy and inexpensive, for you to try: take two cups of rose geranium leaves (all the ingredients must be absolutely dry), one cup each of lemon verbena leaves, sweet woodruff and lavender, and one half cup each of rosemary and thyme. Mix gently and store in an airtight container for six weeks. The resulting blend will be a delicate one, with a subtle hint of fragrance. To make the fragrance stronger, longer-lasting and more noticeable, add two drops each of oil of rose geranium, lavender and lemon verbena, and one drop each of oil of rosemary and thyme to the original mixture, before storing it.

Another pleasant pot-pourri recipe was given to me by Mrs Gregory, wife of the proprietor of the famous rose growers, Gregory's of Nottingham. No exact measurements are given because they are not needed. What is needed is a light hand when adding spices and an extremely light hand when adding oil of roses.

Mrs Gregory's pot-pourri

dried rose petals to form the bulk

dried lavender flowers

mixed, heavily scented dried flowers such as heliotrope,
carnation and honeysuckle

dried, crushed scented leaves, such as mint, sage, fennel,
lemon verbena and scented geranium

freshly grated nutmeg

freshly crushed cloves

freshly grated dried orange and lemon peel

freshly grated allspice (optional)

oil of roses

To dry the flowers, strip the petals and leaves, and place these on a layer of muslin in an airing cupboard or in an oven on the lowest heat, turning them over now and then. If using gas, keep the heat as low as possible and the oven door ajar. The quicker they dry, the quicker the scent will be sealed in. Put the dried petals in a large glass apothecary jar with a tight-fitting lid, in alternating layers if you dried them that way – starting with the most fragrant roses as the first layer. Build up the layers, sprinkling nutmeg and cloves (and allspice, if you are using it) between each layer. Add one or two drops of oil of roses before closing the jar. It is nice to display a quantity in a shallow bowl for visitors; the fragrance will permeate the room.

When pot-pourris start to lose their scent, they can be revived with a few drops of essential oils, ideally the same as those used in the original recipe. Pot-pourris tend to lose their colour, too – first during the drying process and then when they are in open containers, especially when exposed to sunlight. I pep up a visually jaded pot-pourri with a handful of newly dried flower petals, selected purely for colour. I get bright yellow from goldenrod, yarrow, mimosa (expensive I know, but I simply use the dried fluff balls saved from a fresh display), marigolds and black-eyed Susans. Blues and purples come from salvias, pansies and violets, hydrangeas, larkspur and delphiniums. Hydrangeas can also provide a very pretty pink, as does heather and some forms of clematis. Deeply intense colours come from zinnia petals, scarlet sage and the dark mahogany marigolds. White comes from my beloved cow parsley (Queen Anne's lace) and gypsophila.

Fleur Cowles' rose pot-pourri

10 cups dried rose petals

75g (3oz) ground orrisroot

7g ($\frac{1}{2}$oz) each of ground cloves, cinnamon
and allspice

Mix the ingredients thoroughly and store in an earthenware crock for several weeks to mature. Transfer to small
containers to use. You can use this as the basis for variations; different flowers, different spices, dried herbs and
fragrant leaves can all be added, but I am a purist in this
matter and keep strictly to roses.

The container you use to display pot-pourri is just as
important as the ingredients you put into it. Lined baskets
make natural-looking temporary receptacles, or fill a large
conch shell. You might like a finger bowl filled with pot-
pourri at each table setting instead of making a centrepiece. Or make the centrepiece with pot-pourri – stunning! Dress it up with whole dried flowers, or a fresh
flower or two nestled among the dried petals. Lay the bowl
on a bed of leaves and perhaps add a circular garland of
fresh flowers to complete the display. Whatever you use,
remember to spill the pot-pourri carefully back into its
sealed container after the guests have left.

Last-minute pot-pourri news. Recently I learned (and
tested) a 'ten-minute' (or less!) recipe for making pot-
pourri using a microwave oven.

Start with a handful of lemon verbena leaves. Lay them
between two sheets of kitchen paper towelling. Put them
in the microwave oven, set it for two minutes (three may
be too long and could burn the leaves). Take out and lightly
crumble the leaves and set aside in a covered cup or saucer.

Repeat the process with a handful of marigolds or any
other fragrant petals, but do not crumble them.

Repeat the same process with a handful of rose petals
(thick-petalled roses could take up to four minutes), and
again, do not crumble them.

I personally recommend a combination just of roses, marigolds and lemon verbena, but you can add as many flowers
as you wish; do dry each one individually.

When the petals have been baked, gently gather all up and
mix before putting into a covered jar. The lemon verbena
leaves are the 'secret weapon' – absolutely essential for this
deliciously spicy fragrance. However, if you want to add to
the mixture, a few drops of jasmine or a teaspoon of cinnamon, or both, is acceptable.

JARDINIERES AND JAM JARS

I feel the same about containers as I do about flowers: forget all about traditions and what you should and should not do. Not all of the most expensive containers I bought to use as vases were the most useful when it actually came to choosing them for flowers. On the other hand, modest containers destined to spend their lives 'below stairs' serve me well – not that priceless antiques of silver and silver gilt, Venetian glass, marble, alabaster or ormolu haven't also done so! Fabulous ones can look even more so with the right flowers; you simply mustn't let a price tag or classification ('ornamental' or 'kitchenware') interfere with your decision. Snobbery or one-upmanship can get the better of you and your own creativity will be the loser.

POTS AND PANS

In the kitchen there are moulds, cake or bread tins, mixing bowls, mugs, jugs and pitchers waiting to be used – either as they are or dressed up with a coat of paint, moss or fresh leaves (see page 95). This applies not only to today's kitchenware, but to the unloved leftovers of past Victorian or Edwardian eras. If you scour junk shops, market stalls, fairs and jumble sales, you'll soon build up a collection of glazed stoneware storage jars of every shape and dimension, tea caddies, marmalade and ginger pots, spice boxes and – if you're lucky, lovely brass preserving pans, such as the one shown on page 8. Earthenware containers frequently found on bric-à-brac stalls range from the tiny, individual ink pots that sat in old-time school desks to the big, institutional jam jars invaluable for large-scale arrangements. Teapots with missing lids or cracked spouts are worth closer inspection; if they have a nice shape and are not too enthusiastically decorated, buy them for filling with flowers whose leaves will hide the bad spots.

Lower down the kitchen scale are the containers that get thrown away, the discarded soup or vegetable tins, large plastic containers which once held bleach or detergent, and glass jars. Stop throwing them all away; they are the basis of a superb container collection. Those gift packs of four or six tiny jars of marmalade that appear at Christmas-time, emptied of their delicious contents and stripped of their paper labels, make an instant set of containers for small posies. So do jam, pickle, chutney and condiment jars of all shapes and sizes.

DRESSING UP AND SEEING THROUGH

While glass containers need little in the way of enhancement, empty soup tins or plastic bottles (with the top bit carefully removed) need help. Tins of spray paint in a wide selection of colours are the solution. You can mix or match the colour of the container to the colour of its flower occupants with ready-to-use sprays (and change the colour as often as you change its contents). I find that matt sprays tend to fight less with the flowers for your attention than do shiny, high-gloss paint.

Fresh leaves are a surprising but splendid source of disguise. Cake and bread tins, baking sheets and soufflé dishes, as well as the humble containers just mentioned, can be quickly and easily transformed with a 'coat' of leaves. You can do the same 'paste-up' trick by covering the container with moss. If you've dug up moss from your garden, check it first for small creatures before bringing it indoors (it should be insect-free if bought from a florist). Spray mist on leaves and moss-covered containers from time to time to extend their life.

You can glue inexpensive cotton kerchiefs to a dull container to enliven it or simply wrap fabric round the container (tied like a scarf). Fresh-looking cotton gingham is always crisp; so are the simple, old-fashioned printed cottons now popular.

Containers go in and out of fashion in the way that clothes, hair-styles and even flowers do. Not so long ago, books on flower arranging frowned upon glass containers (if books can frown upon anything!). This was because they revealed such contents as crumpled chicken wire, pin holders or plastic foam, and a jumble of crossed stems – which caused particular concern, for to cross stems was forbidden by some traditional flower arrangers. Nowadays crossing stems should be accepted without a second thought. Glass containers still present some minor problems: clear, clean water looks heavenly through glass, and the slight distortion it provides is magical. However, dirty water in a glass container is visually disastrous and even the high-water mark left when the water evaporates isn't pretty. Be prepared to empty out, wash and refill glass containers frequently. To me, there is nothing more elegant than a simple glass container holding tulips; it is worth any extra maintenance effort involved. The slightly imperfect and green-tinted glass of Victorian battery jars (see page 55) is less revealing of murky water – and they are attractive in their own right (once they were easily picked up at junk stores, but now they are making the transition, sadly, to smart antique stores).

Previous page
Silver sand in two shades and pale marble pebbles are used to anchor masses of tulips in a generous and informal display. A chicken wire sub-structure makes arranging the tulips easier, while still allowing the tulips to arch and twist naturally. Once the tulips are in position, carefully pour in sand, top with pebbles and water well. The indoor 'tulip garden' should last for days.

The most valuable and instantly available source of glass containers is the glass (and/or crystal) in your own cabinets. Connoisseurs of wine and those who entertain regularly will have multiples for every possible use: for wine and sherry, for champagne and aperitifs, brandy snifters, tumblers for long, tall drinks and cocktail glasses of every conceivable shape. And all of these can be used singly, in pairs, triplets or as many as you fancy. A limited number of flowers will appear more dramatic if each one is presented individually – given a mini-stage of its own. A dozen carnations in a single vase (quickly absorbed as part of the surroundings) makes a very weak statement. Take those same carnations, cut their stems and float each one in its own brandy glass, and you've made a memorable impression. Cheap and cheerful glasses, if simple and well designed, are every bit as effective as expensive crystal – especially ornate cut crystal, which may sparkle away and gleam with a thousand lights, but also detracts from the flowers in them.

An ephemeral and thoroughly charming 'leaf vase' can be made from an empty soup tin and a generous supply of tough, shiny leaves. Those shown are Portuguese laurel, but elaeagnus or rose leaves would do equally well. Spread the leaf undersides as well as the clean, dry surface of the tin with adhesive, wait for fifteen minutes, then attach the leaves, overlapping them slightly, to the tin. Keep the leaves roughly parallel, and wrap the upper leaves over the rim to complete the disguise. Here tightly bunched blue and white iris, some in bud, some fully open, are 'clasped' by overlapping leaves in a simple, understated display.

The Victorians were immensely fond of ruby-red glass; how exciting it still is to use it for the rich colours of anemones. Perfection! The small, deep blue candle glasses available from religious supply stores are also certainly worth buying; they are exquisite with short-stemmed daisies, mixed bouquets of garden or wild flowers, or crammed full of short roses. Early American milk glass, in pearly, opaque white, is made today and no longer an expensive antique. Bristol glass is very much sought after by collectors, but be

Ordinary drinking glasses can be the neutral basis for variations on a floral theme. Richly coloured De Caen anemones and green-tipped chincherinchees are massed in mixed and single colours, their stark stems providing contrast to the intricate and fragile flower heads. Spotlessly clean glasses and frequent changes of water are essential.

sure the multicoloured speckles and swirls that feature so heavily don't actually work against the beauty of flowers. Those in plain colours are more useful, and are particularly dramatic in blue and deep greens.

Ashtrays of heavy, over-sized hollowed-out cubes of glass, partially filled with water and a bit of plastic foam, are splendid with tightly packed heads of gentians, a blaze of intense blue violets, one fat paeony head, or cheerful yellow winter aconites with ruffled green collars. Because the area of the container is relatively small the outlay on flowers is also small, but the effect is stunning. Place one or more on a low coffee or drinks table and let your guests look down on the flowers.

A word of warning: bud vases are available in glass or crystal, traditionally for displaying a single rose. Besides being a little too predictable many have the additional drawback of instability. They are so tall and thin that the weight of a fully opened rose (and remember, buds do open eventually) may be enough to send them toppling over. Do use them for clematis, or even honeysuckle; neither has much weight and both are so elegant.

WEAVES AND WOODS

No one can have too many baskets. I never travel without looking for new weaves, new shapes, new colours – and all are among the least expensive of containers. They've been around for so many years that they've bypassed fads and fashions – they're 'in' forever as far as I'm concerned. They look absolutely right in almost every setting: tiny ones can be used for tiny pots of flowers, big ones give a home to armfuls of wild flowers, autumn leaves or winter berries and stems, all sitting in a hidden container of water within the woven basket.

I am always on the look-out for baskets with open-work designs which I line with gingham or bright calico to be seen through the holes in the weave (flowers go into jars concealed in the basket). My favourite ones include friendly black-eyed Susans, vivid pompon chrysanthemums and marigolds. Smaller baskets can be filled with violets (or even cheerful dandelions which I always pick because I don't believe they deserve being snubbed).

Changing the scale: big woven baskets, such as those intended to hold logs or kindling by a fireplace, or even to hold laundry, are worth a second look. With a bucket of water inside, and the lid removed or left in an open position, they make superb holders for huge rhubarb flowers, masses of dried acanthus, branches of autumn leaves, or, my favourite, cow parsley (Queen Anne's lace).

I change the colour of baskets as quickly and as easily as I do the colour of tins and plastic bottles, using spray paints. A woven, wine red basket filled with pale pink and deep, wine red roses is a real show stopper. Try it. Or deep green, filled with masses of variegated leaves. The possible combinations are endless. Fishermen's woven bags (with hidden containers of water inside) can be left open on a table with flowers spilling out where one might expect to see tackle or bait. Woven oriental boxes – square, round or rectangular – make homes for either modest or lush large-scale displays.

The simple split-wood baskets in which fruit and berries are sometimes sold, or wooden kitchen garden trugs such as the one used on page 52, and even old cigar boxes, look right on gingham tablecloths in the kitchen but are also charming on the luncheon table. Consider using wooden salad bowls, both the large serving sort and small individual ones. To keep them in perfect condition, line them carefully with silver foil before filling with plastic foam, or better still put shallow, water-filled containers inside.

TALLS AND SMALLS

Umbrella stands, abandoned and standing forlorn in entrance halls, need to be looked at with new eyes. Forget about umbrellas, for a little while anyway, and fill them with hollyhocks, delphiniums, big branches of glistening crab apples or any large-scale, generous material that catches your fancy. In spring, try branches of horse chestnut or sycamore; their unfurling foliage and buds are exquisite. In autumn, their dying colours are equally riveting. If the stand is open-topped, insert a container for water. If it is the sort with holes into which the umbrellas fit, use it dry for a short-term but glorious display. The informality – even gentle humour – of the idea will be much appreciated by guests as they arrive.

Waste-paper baskets (even those in rigid plastic, cylindrical form) come in clear, bright colours and even black. Use them for dramatic floor displays. If the idea that they are normally humble waste containers doesn't 'sit' right with you, use lots of trailing ivy or other foliage to obscure their true identity, or cover the outside with large leaves gummed to the surface.

Although I admire the skilful and delicate work involved in minuscule arrangements, they require so many technical tricks that I generally avoid them. Sometimes, however, I do use small round antique silver or modern glass salt cellars, filling either with such treasures as aubretia or arabis. A small (but not minute) shell packed with plastic foam

Umbrella stands make humorous and unexpected 'homes' for tall-stemmed hollyhocks. With wicker or other non-waterproof stands, use an inner, waterproof container. It will probably be necessary to raise the level, so rest it on a built-up layer of newspapers. A light-weight stand will need a heavy object in the bottom, to prevent it tipping over.

can display a mixture of pinks and heathers. You can recycle empty perfume jars; a great deal of care and lots of money have been spent on their design, and it is silly not to make use of them. Empty medicine bottles, free of labels and with one small flower in each, are much more humble, but no less appealing if used in a row parading across a bathroom windowsill. Try to collect an assortment of blues, browns and yellows, if you can. The back light will set the flowers and coloured glass off beautifully.

DO'S AND DON'TS

◆ *Do* make up your mind about what you like in the way of containers.

◆ *Don't* be bound by other people's rules of proportion. I don't, and never will. Why not try a tall glass spaghetti jar filled with tightly packed Peruvian lilies *(Alstroemeria)*? Why not try a huge sunflower head larger in size than the soup plate it is in – or in a shallow glass bowl? All of these contradict the proportion rules, and all are stunning. Keep balance in mind for practicality's sake; a container filled with a top-heavy arrangement is a danger to itself and everything around it, including people and nearby furniture. Plastic and fibreglass containers are particularly hazardous because they are so light in weight. If you use them, weigh them down with stones or sand.

◆ *Don't* be put off by porousness. Nearly everything can be made usable by a smaller waterproof container or bit of plastic foam wrapped in polythene inside.

◆ *Do* keep your containers clean – this is a must. Water at room temperature is a haven for bacteria, and a container that is dirty to begin with gives bacteria a head start. Soap and water plus mild disinfectant will do the clean-up trick, or try the traditional mixtures of lemon juice and salt or a handful of sand to scour away stains.

◆ *Do* play the numbers game with containers. Lots of small containers, such as the elegant Victorian Parian porcelain shown on page 35 can look superb. Six cups and saucers, whether expensive porcelain or rough pottery, can be filled with only a handful of flowers and drunk with the eyes.

◆ *Do* keep your sense of humour. A child's open toy car can be filled with damp plastic foam and bright-centred daisies. A simple chamber pot will receive a second life when disguised by nasturtiums and their overspilling leaves.

◆ *Do* mix and match. The illustrations on pages 102–3 show the same flowers – sea holly *(Eryngium)* and single yellow chrysanthemums – in very different containers: four

For a summer luncheon party, indoors or out, put a waterproof, flat-bottomed container in the crown of a wide-brimmed straw hat. Fill with tightly packed flowers, such as a mixture of salmon, pink and bright red geraniums. Use pretty leaves to hide any gaps and make a ruffle round the edge, and trail a matching satin ribbon over the table or tablecloth.

rustic, hand-painted pottery jars, and one large Portuguese glazed enamel basket. Two different feelings have been created, the first refreshingly informal, the second rather more formal. Try a series of identical containers, using slightly different combinations of flowers or colours in each, as shown on page 96.

◆ *Do* let inventiveness win out over tradition and economy. If you lack the funds for a glazed jardiniere (and let's admit it, they are spectacular!) buy a huge clay flower-pot instead. For a fraction of the cost, and with a water-proof container inside, you can now display flowers on just as grand a scale. I happen to love the naturalness of clay.

◆ *Don't* let containers and contents fight with each other. If you have a gorgeous cachepot heavily decorated with

These four mini-arrangements contain the same flowers – yellow and white chrysanthemums and steel-blue sea holly – as the large bouquet (facing page). The rustic, hand-painted pottery jars, each holding a tight cluster and marching in an orderly procession across the surface, convey an entirely different feeling from the exuberant and deliciously haphazard mass

of flowers in the glazed ceramic basket. Neither is 'better' than the other, and both display equally simple approaches to using cut flowers.

painted flowers, fill it with a mass of fresh foliage and let the flowers be provided by those on the container itself (page 63). Neutral containers take the widest range of flower colours, but if you can *exactly* match a particular vase to a particular flower colour, the effect is stunning – like a spray of yellow orchids in a yellow ceramic vase, or white roses in fine white china.

◆ Don't ever consider your collection of containers complete. Be on the look-out, always, for new containers to add to your collection. Ones you've had for years that are starting to bore you can be stored for a while, or disposed of, if you lack storage space. New containers often challenge your imagination, thus improving your floral skills.

LIFE-LONG TECHNIQUES

Decorating with flowers may be an art, but there is a little bit of science involved, too. Once you have acquired the very few tools and technical skills set out below – and these are all the ones that I've found most useful over the years – you'll be able to create exactly the arrangement you have in your mind's eye. Just as importantly, you'll get the longest life (and most pleasure!) from the flowers and foliage after they're arranged, and you'll have the additional satisfaction of knowing that *your* time, effort and initial outlay are giving maximum returns.

A LONGER LIFE FOR CUT FLOWERS
Keeping cut flowers alive and attractive for as long as possible is crucial because all the creativity in the world won't make up for flowers and foliage that have wilted prematurely. My interest in this problem began long, long ago, when I was faced with the special problem of poppies. I found their charm irresistible and longed to use them in bouquets, but their papery petals wilted and faded in my hand as soon as they were cut. I became determined to learn how to prolong their life, and from this determination came a life-long study. Over the years, I read books on the subject, asked for advice, experimented, bullied friends to extract information, collected ideas and comments, and added this wealth of knowledge to my own personal experience.
Keeping cut flowers alive longer is an art as well as a science but it also depends on common sense. As with any acquired skill, there are fads, fashions and passing theories to sift through and assess. Equally respected books on the subject by eminent authors may give radically different instructions on prolonging the life of a particular flower or on the effectiveness of using a particular chemical. I am including whatever methods have worked best for me over many years of dealing with flowers.

BUYING THE BEST
Most people rely entirely on their florist or local flower stall as a source of material. Those fortunate enough to have their own cutting gardens still find it necessary to rush to the florist from time to time, especially in the winter months or when a summer storm has rendered

useless the most beautiful of garden flowers. If you have made a friend of a reliable florist and have shown that you are seriously interested in flowers, the chances are that you'll be very well looked after, so it really is worthwhile to find the best florist you can and stick to him or her. But it is always valuable to know the tell-tale signs of a fresh and not-so-fresh flower.

Odd as it may seem, looking at the stems and leaves can be as revealing as looking at the flowers themselves. Slimy, smelly or discoloured stems are to be avoided, together with leaves that are wilted, faded, spotted or yellowed. A good florist would never allow flowers in this state to be sold. Flowers are 'cleaned' and prepared before going on display, and these tell-tale signs are sometimes removed. This test, and the following generalities, will help you judge for yourself. Make sure stems are crisp and bright looking and hard rather than soft. Don't buy flowers that are drooping or bending at the neck. You may be able to revive them (advice on page 115) but it is far better to buy fresh material than to attempt a rescue operation. Next, check the texture of the petals. While some, such as scabious, are naturally paper thin, any sign of transparency in the normally opaque petals of lilies, daffodils, stocks and the lower edge of arum lilies, for example, is a sign of old age. Colour changes are slightly trickier. Any darkening around the edge of the petals or in the centre of the flower can be a sign of age, though some flowers – many roses, for instance – have a naturally dark edge to the petals. Some flowers grow paler as they grow older – cornflowers change from rich deep blue to pale blue-grey. Experience will soon show you how to interpret the colour of any particular flower.

Whether to buy flowers in bud or fully open has long been a subject of controversy. If given the option, I always prefer to choose a flower that is just starting to open, to avoid the risk of the bud refusing to open at all while still getting full benefit of its flowering life. Unfortunately, florists rarely have flowers at that optimum stage of development, and we have to make compromises. As a general rule, sprays of flowers such as pinks or spray carnations should have masses of fat buds just starting to show colour, with a few actually open. A quick but thorough glance will tell you whether any dying flower heads have been snipped off; one or two won't matter, but the more empty stalks there are, the less flowers for you. Tightly shut green buds rarely fulfil their promise, though paeonies can be bought in bud with little risk of failure. Roses, tulips, iris, daffodils and gladioli are considered safe flowers to buy in bud too,

Previous page
A fragile and generous display of clematis, individually in glass candlesticks and massed in a central, stemmed glass dish. Clematis are notoriously difficult as cut flowers and, unless treated – or conditioned – immediately after being cut, wilt almost instantly. By singeing the cut stem, though, and completely submerging the flower in lukewarm water for a few hours, you can dramatically extend its life as a cut flower. Removing the leaves helps, too; if you want to mix leaves and flowers, as shown here, add the flowerless leaf stalks separately.

While some cut flowers will last almost in spite of neglect, there are many flowers besides clematis, and much foliage, that benefit enormously from initial conditioning.

though I prefer to have a range of stages – some buds, some newly opened flowers, perhaps even a fully opened one – just as you find them in nature, rather than from a 'factory production line'.

Flowers that grow on long stems, such as delphiniums and gladioli, open from the bottom of the stem upwards. Flowers missing from the bottom means they've bloomed and died – another discouraging sign.

Lastly, look at the centres of the flowers. Daisy-like flowers, such as single chrysanthemums, pyrethrums, shasta daisies and rudbeckias, should have hard centres, with little, if any, pollen visible. Soft centres with masses of pollen mean the flowers are well on the way to completing their reproductive cycles and fading. Double flowers – chrysanthemums especially – should have tightly packed centres, with just slightly looser petals round the rim. Reflexed chrysanthemums have petals which curve naturally under and towards the stem, and spider chrysanthemums are shaggy and dishevelled by nature; but pompon chrysanthemums that have loose and limp petals around the edge are not worth buying.

Ask your florist to wrap any flowers with large or delicate heads individually, for safe transport home. And don't make the fatal mistake of abandoning your carefully selected flowers to the back seat of a hot or freezing cold car while you spend hours shopping. It is far better to pick your flowers up last.

If you can find any *galax* leaves (you can in America), buy them as an investment. These and cycas leaves remain alive long after the flowers they accompany die, indeed almost forever if you keep them in a plastic bag in a refrigerator. They are pretty on a dining table, making a design around a bowl of flowers, or pasted around ordinary containers. They also make a good ruffle around a bouquet, softening hard edges. Eucalyptus are other long-term foliage investments, and will last through several flower arrangements, though I personally find them a little too aromatic.

FIRST PICK

Picking flowers from my garden is always a great treat; the seasonal changes are far more apparent than they are in any florist's shop, and small treasures reveal themselves in every nook and cranny. Though the time lapse between picking and arranging is inevitably shorter than between buying already cut flowers and arranging, do follow these sensible guidelines.

When to pick? This is another highly controversial subject, even in learned books. Some advocate cutting flowers in the morning, when their water content is highest, but I prefer the early evening, when their food reserves are highest. The flowers then spend the night in a deep bath laced with the Cut Flower Nutrient described on page 112. Logically, a morning pick means the flowers spend all day in water and should be arranged that *evening,* which to me makes little sense to tired or busy people. Most books advise against picking flowers in the heat of the midday sun and I agree, but if you have no choice get the flowers into water quickly.

Taking an old-fashioned flower trug or wicker basket round the garden makes for splendid imagery, but unfortunately the flowers collected in them are drying out the whole time. Less attractive but far more sensible is a big plastic bucket, one third full of water (more will make it heavy and unwieldy).

When cutting, consider the plant you are leaving behind. With trees and shrubs, this becomes a double exercise: pruning as well as obtaining material for using indoors. You may have to compromise between the branch most heavily laden with flowers, foliage or berries, and the one which is perhaps less luscious but really more suitable because its absence won't destroy the overall look of the plant. Make your cut just above a node so that new shoots will be encouraged to form, with no die-back of the woody stump. Cutting annuals and perennials, far from denuding the garden, encourages the production of more flowers, but do try to leave some buds on the remaining plant to give some colour until the next lot of buds has formed.

Always make your cuts on a slant; this gives the largest surface through which water can be absorbed. With carnations and pinks, make the cut 2.5cm (1in) above or below a node, as it is difficult for water to be absorbed into the stem through the nodes.

CONDITIONING

Whether you are dealing with florists' flowers or those fresh from your garden, the few minutes spent in conditioning the flowers will reward you with days of extra pleasure. It is important to understand the theory and the general rules behind conditioning before attempting to deal with specific problems and all of the many exceptions. Basically, when a flower is cut, a callus forms over the cut surface, preventing the intake of water and thus hastening wilting. In addition, air locks form behind the callus, causing additional blockage. The types of conditioning listed below all counteract this blockage, and result in water being freely available to the stem.

Whichever technique you use, first remove all foliage and shoots that will be below or just above the water line in the container. Submersion quickly rots the leaves and shoots, and encourages the formation of bacteria which can block the flower stems. The leaves of some flowers such as dahlias, lilacs and philadelphus take far more water from the stem than is good for the flowers, which rapidly wilt. Completely strip the leaves from these, above and below the water line, to extend the life of the bloom. If you do want to arrange the flowers with their own leaves, add a few leafy, non-flowering stems. Since most of the leaves of the plants I mentioned are quite ordinary – even dull looking – try using more attractive leaves instead.

Another absolute rule is to re-cut flowers, whether from your garden or a shop, at the start of conditioning. Make the cut at a slant, 2.5cm (1in) above the previous cut and, if at all possible, have the stem submerged while you make the cut, to prevent the formation of an airlock.

Hollow stems: treat the hollow stems of large dahlias, delphiniums and lupins as miniature water containers. Simply turn the cut stem upside down, fill it to the top with water, and plug the end with a bit of cotton wool. The latter acts as a sponge, drawing up more water as that within the stem is absorbed.

Bleeding stems: euphorbia, with its glorious grey-green foliage, poppies, heliotropes, and dandelions among the wild flowers exude a milky sap that can block the intake of water. Singe the cut surface over a match or candle flame until the end is blackened. Alternatively, dip it in boiling water for 30 seconds. After searing, transfer to a large container of cool water.

Woody stems: all flowering shrubs – camellias, rhododendrons, lilacs, hydrangeas – should have the bottom 5cm (2in) of their stems split or crushed, to help them absorb water better. Next, scrape away another 5cm (2in) of bark, immediately above the crushed portion. Place the cut ends in a shallow container of boiling water for 30 seconds, then transfer immediately to a large container of cool water. It is a good idea to protect the flower heads from the rising steam during the immersion in boiling water. Place the heads in polythene bags or cut small holes in a sheet of newspaper, slip the stem through, and secure the newspaper in a bag-like fashion around the head.

Soft stems: these need no special treatment except re-cutting under water, followed by a long, cool soak.

Foliage: except for silver, grey and woolly leaved foliage, which dislike any water on the leaves, totally submerge foliage in a bucket of cold water overnight.

Bulbs: because bulbs can take in water from the green portion of the stem only, cut off any white at the base of the stem. Additionally, daffodils, narcissi and hyacinths tend to leak white fluid from the cut surface. Wash this off thoroughly in cool running water.

As with any rules, there are bound to be exceptions and qualifications. The following are a few examples from my list of popular flowers, both from the garden and the florist, which need slightly special treatment.

Allium: despite the huge and beautiful flower heads, these are members of the onion family and unfortunately the typical onion smell is very persistent. Wrap the stems in cotton wool dampened with water and mild disinfectant, then enclose them in a waterproof polythene bag before placing in a container with other flowers. Incidentally, this same treatment is useful for ornamental cabbage plants: wrap the roots in damp cotton wool and polythene.

Amaryllis: if you can bear to cut the bloom from this majestic plant (I can't), do so while it is in the bud stage, with the buds showing colour. It needs the hollow stem treatment (see above). Be extremely careful when handling the stem, because the flower heads have a tendency to snap off. A thin stick can also be inserted into the stem, to help support the weight of the flower-head.

Berries: these have as much beauty as flowers, and a potentially long life. Remove the leaves, split and scrape the stems as for all woody plants, then submerge them completely for their first night. I was once told to spray them with plastic or hair spray to keep them firm and on the stems longer but this I prefer not to do.

Camellia: these flowers, like amaryllis, all too often snap off at the base, so be very careful when handling them. Never touch the flowers directly, or brush one against another, or they easily bruise and turn brown. To condition those on short stems, lay them in a tissue box on a bed of wet cotton wool. Cover with additional wet cotton wool, spray with cool water and keep overnight in a cool place.

Chrysanthemum: the foliage of chrysanthemums has a much shorter cut life than that of the flowers, so remove all or most of it. Though it is technically a herbaceous perennial, the stems are very woody. The bottom 7.5-10cm (3-4in) of stem should be scraped with a sharp knife to remove the outer skin, and the remaining skinned stem split. Incidentally, this treatment is best for Michaelmas daisies and heathers, too.

Clematis: admittedly tricky, it is nevertheless worth trying to condition these magnificent flowers. Remove all the leaves and either singe the cut stem with a lighted match or candle or submerge completely in lukewarm water for a couple of hours.

Gladiolus: snip off the tiny buds at the top of the stem as they rarely open. Snap off flowers as they die.

Hellebore: like clematis, hellebores are alluringly beautiful, but can be difficult to condition. Place the cut tip of the stem in boiling water for 30 seconds, then immerse the entire stem in warm water for several hours. Splitting the stem also helps the flow of water to the flower, and using a container deep enough totally to submerge the stems in water is advisable.

Mimosa is sold in polythene bags for good reason. The fluffy yellow heads are quick to mature; they soon shed their pollen and die. After crushing and boiling the stem-tips in the usual way, soak the stems overnight in water, with the flower heads still encased in polythene. Display the flowers in a cool room, if possible.

Roses: remove the thorns with a sharp knife as part of the conditioning process.

Tulips: tulip stems have a habit of arching, twisting and turning in graceful ways. If you prefer all the stems to be erect (I don't), wrap the tulips, flower-heads and all, in a few sheets of newspaper secured with an elastic band. Place the parcel in a deep bucket of water overnight, and by the following morning the stems will have 'set' straight. If you want both erect and curving tulips, treat only half this way; put the rest in water just as they are for the night.

Violets: I prefer starting with fully opened violets, as those picked in bud never open for me. Submerge the flowers in cool water for an hour (or put them face down in water each night, as I do). The water is then absorbed by the flowers as well as the stems, and this technique keeps them crisp and fresh. Incidentally, I also give the underwater treatment to magnolias, whenever I am lucky enough to obtain cut branches in flower.

AFTERCARE

Let's assume your flowers and foliage have been bought or cut in the peak of health, carefully conditioned and placed in their containers. You may think that your responsibilities are over; they are not. It is more a question of sensitivity and awareness of the continuing needs of flowers and foliage than long, hard work, so don't be discouraged.

Before placing the container in the visually most appropriate place in the room, first consider the health and long life of its contents. Draughts spell death to flowers; air movement dries out the petals and foliage faster than the

Violets take in water through their flower petals as well as through their stems. Immediately after picking, completely submerge them in water for an hour, to give them a long, cool drink. And if you display violets on their own, in a simple bunch, as I often do, repeat the exercise every night to refresh and invigorate the flowers. Tying the stems in a rubber band first will keep the bunch tidy.

stems can replace the lost water. Heat (or excess heat, to be specific) is another mortal enemy, so avoid south- or west-facing windowsills in summer, or positions near fireplaces and radiators.

Check and fill the containers daily, even twice a day if necessary. Dry atmosphere can have much the same effect as dry containers, so mist the arrangement regularly but gently. Don't aim the spray directly at the flowers and foliage; spray the air above them, and let the mist settle of its own accord. Misting is especially important for branches of flowering shrubs such as camellias and rhododendrons (but not the white ones), which aren't particularly good at absorbing water through their stems. Don't mist grey or woolly leaves, or such waxy-petalled flowers as gardenias and lilies, which quickly stain and discolour. Snip out dead flower heads and any dead or dying foliage.

CUT FLOWER NUTRIENT

Whether or not additives – aspirin, sugar, alcohol, vinegar, disinfectant, even lemonade – actually prolong the life of cut flowers is a controversial subject. Some very seasoned arrangers swear by them; others treat the whole business of adding chemicals to water in a container as one big fraud. I compare this controversy to that over herbalism: there is some truth in these old-fashioned folkloric remedies, and so there is in the floral equivalent of modern medicine. Proprietary nutrients available from florists and additives you might have in your cupboards at home all have their uses.

The following formula was originally developed by professional rose growers to prolong the life of roses and all flowers during exhibitions. It has been scientifically proven and tested.

1 part salt

1 part potassium chloride

4 parts alum

60 parts glucose

Mix the ingredients thoroughly and add 15ml (1tbsp) to 600ml (1pt) water. Make more solution than you require at any one time, and use the rest for refilling your container. I place the flower stems directly into this solution for their overnight conditioning drink.

Of the old-fashioned solutions, aspirin dissolved in water is probably the most universally used, together with sugar dissolved in water. One aspirin and a small spoonful of

With one or two exceptions, cut flowers should be misted regularly with lukewarm water, to help prolong their lives. Never mist from point-blank range; try to aim slightly above the flowers, so the moisture falls gently down of its own accord. sugar in a medium-size vase is the standard recipe. The sugar feeds the flowers and the aspirin reduces water loss through leaves. Charcoal or alum is used to keep the water clear. A tiny bit of bleach or general disinfectant keeps the growth of bacteria down (and the stench of decomposition as well). The Japanese swear by pure alcohol, as a conditioner rather than in the final container; they put the stems of water lilies and clematis in it for a few minutes before transferring them to their containers. I find that water lilies stay open best if you carefully drip melting wax between the petals to 'fix' them.

SPECIAL PROBLEMS

Because I drive to London after country weekends, I have of necessity mastered the art of transporting flowers. Enclosed in airtight transparent plastic, they make their own moist mini-environment and will come to no harm. If it is cold out, a second covering of several thicknesses of newspaper keeps them warm. For large branches, I use a bucket with a few inches of water in the bottom on the floor at the back of the car. Make sure the bucket is wedged firmly, though, and is not too full of water.

Never discard a floral display out of hand. More often than not, some of the flowers and leaves will have a second life – or even a third – if you judiciously re-cut their stems, give them fresh water and a smaller container. The large arrangement of flowers and foliage (*left*) includes Barberton daisies, gypsophila, acanthus, leafless branches of crab apples, seed pods, and senecio, rhododendron and cotinus foliage.

A week later, this scaled-down, but still lovely posy (*right*), was made from the remains of the larger arrangement. Far from being a shameful exercise, making new arrangements from old means that you take your flowers seriously and enjoy the creative challenge they present.

Revival techniques are essential. Your heart may leap at the arrival of an expensive-looking box or wrapped bunch of flowers on your doorstep, only to sink when you see the state of the flowers themselves. It isn't necessarily the fault of the florist; the flowers may have left the shop in perfect condition but spent too long in the back of the delivery van. Don't despair. Cut the stems again, under water, place the stem ends in boiling water for 30 seconds, protecting the flower heads if necessary, then give the stems a long, tall drink of warm water for several hours.

This is also a very good technique to try with flowers that were fresh to start with but have wilted after having given a few days' service in an arrangement at home.

Though it may seem odd to include instructions on keeping flowers from opening in a chapter devoted to keeping them open longer, it really is just another aspect of the same skill. If you are giving a big party, for example, and your flowers are delivered two or three days in advance, store them in a cool (but not freezing), dark place. A refrigerator can be a bit too cold if set at its coldest. If you do use one, wrap the flowers in polythene first.

SECOND-HAND ROSE

Because flowers are so very expensive to buy and because I am a naturally economy-minded person, I very rarely consign an entire arrangement to the dustbin. Flowers have different natural life spans, whether growing or cut; it is my standard procedure to go over them, extracting those with life still in them to use to make a scaled-down display. The arrangements on pages 114 and 115 show one such exercise. Stems can be shortened (especially if they show any sign of sliminess) and sprays taken apart into single flowers and buds. Faded outer petals, such as those of paeony, chrysanthemum and dahlia, can be removed (using fine manicure scissors or tweezers), leaving an inner core of relatively fresh petals.

Certain flowers are almost always worth a second go; among the most long lasting are chrysanthemum, foxtail lilies (Eremurus), gladioli, sea holly (Eryngium), chincherinchee (Ornithogalum) – which last for weeks without wilting – Peruvian lily (Alstroemeria), globe thistle (Echinops), and statice. Good long-lasting leaves include evergreen berberis, camellia, eucalyptus, Garrya elliptica, bergenia, Portuguese laurel, eleagnus and New Zealand flax (Phormium). On the other side of the coin, enjoy for their brief but glorious beauty such short-lived treasures as passion flowers, acanthus, mimosa, lupins, bluebells and young beech leaves. Bamboo also has a fresh but transient charm, although it does dry well for use with other dried flowers.

TOOLS AND TECHNICALITIES

Having the right tools and knowing exactly how to use them is as essential as the containers or flowers themselves. However, what you mustn't do is become a slave to technical skills, such as keeping an unbelievably high fruit and floral masterpiece from toppling, for example, forcing flowers into contorted geometric arrangements or wiring up the naturally graceful, curving stem of a tulip into rigid, straight perfection. Never confuse techniques with creativity; the simplest and most natural solution is often the best one. For this reason, I've kept the check-list of equipment and techniques below as short as possible.

Plastic foam: though there are several proprietary forms available, Oasis is probably the best known. There is one sort for dried flower arrangements (polystyrene is an alternative) which can be used again and again until it finally disintegrates; the other sort retains water when soaked, allowing the use of containers that would otherwise be too shallow to hold sufficient water. If the foam is covered with aluminium foil or clear plastic wrap, even porous containers can be used for flowers. Both types support the flower stems at whatever angle they are inserted, but do use a certain amount of caution: the results can sometimes be oddly angular and unnatural-looking. Plastic foam comes in various pre-formed shapes which include large rectangular blocks that can be cut to the exact shape you want. It is invaluable for making such things as floral balls, in which case wrapping it in chicken wire gives it added strength.

When soaking plastic foam for use with fresh flowers, wait until the bubbles stop rising to the water surface, and if possible add water to the container as well. Don't forget to keep a check on the moisture level in the plastic foam, as it can dry out just as quickly as the water in any flower arrangement. Regular misting with a spray will help. Keep in mind the fact that some plants – anemones, spring-flowering bulbs, grey and silver foliage, violets and forget-me-nots, for example – cannot make proper use of the water held by the plastic foam, even when fully saturated. They should be used in containers that can hold extra water. Some flowers have stems too soft to insert – a problem that can be solved by making holes with an awl or dowel, or by tying several of the soft stems together and attaching them to a stick which is then inserted firmly into the plastic foam.

Chicken wire: this has the advantage of lasting virtually forever and is very useful for supporting heavy branches and flower stems in water. Buy the 5cm (2in) mesh; anything smaller becomes impenetrable when crumpled. There should be enough 'crumple' to give three or four layers of wire for stems to pass through, and the mass of wire must fit snugly in the container (if not, the flowers will move about). When using a wide container, you may find that bending the edges over the rim helps to keep the wire securely in position. If the container has handles or a spout, you can secure the chicken wire by passing string or tightly stretched rubber bands across the top of the container.

Unlike plastic foam, chicken wire won't necessarily support a stem exactly as it is inserted, and a certain amount of settlement usually takes place. While some people find this a hindrance, I prefer the slight challenge involved, and like the natural look of the resulting arrangement of flowers.

Flower holders: there are basically two sorts of holders for flowers, glass and metal. Glass flower holders are a Victorian invention – dome-shaped, with a series of holes into which the stems fit. Because the holes are so formally arranged, the finished appearance is liable to have an equally formal, unnatural-looking regularity, rather like the radiating spokes of a wheel. Try using a glass holder to support the main framework of flowers, but fill in the framework with enough foliage or smaller flowers to offset and counteract the rigid formality. A word of warning: never attempt to jam tough, woody stems into glass holders, because the glass between the individual holes is often quite thin and could break.

Metal pinholders do the same job as glass flower holders, usually with less rigid-looking results. The best are made of heavy metal and can be expensive, but they do last for ever and are worth the initial investment. The metal bases are closely packed with nails on which the stems are impaled, and come in various sizes; large, with widely spaced nails for woody stems, or small, fine and dense for delicate stems; there are very fine ones for tiny bouquets. Don't buy plastic pinholders, as they are too lightweight to be of any practical use.

For extra stability, both glass and metal holders can be fixed to the base of containers with three small balls of plasticine (which you should include in your check-list of equipment). Make sure that the container, holder and plasticine are all absolutely dry, otherwise the plasticine won't adhere. Both types of holder can also be used with chicken wire for additional support, and both should be kept scrupulously clean and dry when not in use.

Secateurs and scissors: don't use ordinary scissors, which tend to crush stems. Florists' scissors have serrated edges and are much better, though a pair of small scissors is useful for removing leaves, thorns and wilted flower heads. Sharp secateurs are essential for cutting woody branches from the garden or shortening the tough, woody stems of chrysanthemums and roses. A sharp knife is handy for stripping the bark from the bases of certain plants during the initial conditioning.

Wire: though I am firmly against using florists' wire to perform miraculous feats of engineering, or to wire flowers into unnatural shapes, it can be useful for splinting together the broken stem of a flower, adding length to a short flower stem or fixing into position small mushrooms and kumquats in vegetable, fruit and flower arrangements.

Plasticine: besides its usefulness in fixing flower holders to containers, plasticine is the perfect tool to build up and fill out a container that is too big. Thin slivers of plasticine can also be used to support fruit and vegetables in arrangements. Use it sparingly to secure what should be a natural-looking arrangement, and don't try to challenge the laws of gravity; the results never look right.

Mister: mist spraying is essential to refresh cut flowers and foliage. Using a light touch, spray above the bouquet and let the drops of mist settle on the flowers and foliage beneath, protecting the furniture, if necessary.

Bucket and watering can: for collecting flowers from the garden, or storing them until they are used, buckets are invaluable. A small watering can with a long thin spout is essential for refilling arrangements, as water rapidly evaporates in warm rooms and is taken up by the flower or foliage stems. The long spout allows you to manoeuvre well into the container without disturbing the flowers or risking spillage.

Florist's vials: these are an absolute must. They are clear plastic or metal miniature containers which are filled with water, and topped with open-centered rubber lids through which the cut stem is pushed. Orchids are often sold with florist's vials already attached. Keep them and use them in many ways. They will extend the life of individual flowers inserted between fruit or vegetables in mixed displays, or tucked into pot plants, and you can use them to insert short-stemmed flowers into a large bouquet of long-stemmed flowers.

Candle cups: small metal cups can be bought to fit over candlesticks (which I often use in the daytime for flowers); they hold enough water to support flowers and foliage, or if necessary a small piece of plastic foam can be used. Don't worry if the cups have an 'added on' look, as they can be concealed by trailing or arching foliage and flowers. As with flower holders in the base of containers, candle cups can be fixed into position with plasticine, but first make sure that all the components are dry.

Awl: this small pointed tool is useful for making the preliminary holes in plastic foam if you are inserting soft-stemmed flowers. Thin pencils and nails are equally good alternatives, depending on the thickness of the stem.

Adhesives: as well as plasticine, double-sided tape, paste and Cow Gum glue are necesary tools, The asparagus shown on page 51 were attached to the container with double-sided tape, and paste and glue are equally useful for fixing attractive leaves to otherwise unattractive containers (see page 95).

Sand, pebbles and stones: these are intriguing additions to use as a base in transparent containers. Irises are particularly nice when wedged between stones, so are tulips (see page 92). Sand, pebbles or stones, whether visible (they *are* pleasant to see) or hidden, help to stabilize lightweight containers, and can also raise the bottom of exceptionally tall containers if you want to use short-stemmed flowers. Pinholders or glass flower holders in a shallow container can be concealed with any of the above.

Moss: this deserves mentioning here even though it is a living plant. There are three main types of moss, each with special qualities. Bun moss is the green, velvety moss you can dig up from your garden or buy from a florist. Use it

An antique white tablecloth makes a charming background for a bed of moss, which in turn becomes the backdrop for a bouquet of white roses. A baking tray protects the tablecloth from the moss, and a shallow glass dish, embedded in the moss, holds the roses.

in a shallow dish as a stage setting for spring-flowering bulbs, primroses or violets which can be dug up, roots and all, given a temporary, mossy home indoors and then returned to the garden for a quick recovery. Use moss to conceal compost in a potted plant, or glue it to the outside of any unattractive container.

Sphagnum, Spanish or sheet moss, which grows in damp, acid bogs and heaths, is also available from florists. Sphagnum moss holds water like a sponge, and thus was a natural precursor to plastic foam. It can be used in much the same way: to support the stems of cut flowers and foliage, and to provide a source of water in an otherwise dry environment, such as a floral ball or wreath. Like plastic foam, it should be thoroughly soaked before use and regularly replenished with a watering can or mist spray. To pack a frame with moss, take handfuls of well-dampened, live sphagnum moss and push it firmly into position around the frame. Dried sphagnum moss looks a bit like hay: use it to cover up and conceal kitchen containers. It also looks well as a base for a glass bowl of flowers.

Reindeer, or lichen, moss is a beautiful silvery-grey colour but, unlike the other two, is dead and dried by the time it reaches the florist. Some soak it before using it to conceal the base of a pot plant or to decorate leafless twigs and branches in winter arrangements. I also use it dry to decorate the soil in potted plants.

Artificial moss is available from some florists, but it looks as unnatural as it sounds. Avoid using it. Natural moss, when not in use, should be stored in an airtight plastic bag in the refrigerator.

FLORAL BALLS

It is easier to make a floral ball from dried flowers than from fresh, although I use both with success. With dried flowers, you need not work against the clock, as the flowers are not in any danger of wilting. That having been said, the absolute splendour of a floral ball made of *fresh* flowers is worth all the technical bother and risk involved. Securely perched on dowel 'trunks' (which can then be hidden by ivy or ribbons), floral balls make the perfect table companion for an elegant dinner party. They allow conversation to flow and guests' faces to be seen beneath them, while their ephemeral quality – here today, gone tomorrow or, if not tomorrow, not long thereafter – emphasizes the importance of the occasion. You might hang a floral ball on a satin ribbon in front of a mirror to double the beauty of the original by reflection, such as the one shown on page 123.

To make the ball foundation for use with fresh flowers, cut the plastic foam into a roughly circular shape, saturate it, then drain it thoroughly until it no longer drips. If the ball is to have a larger diameter than the width of the block of plastic foam, pack together several pieces to form a composite ball. Wrap the piece (or pieces) in tin foil, then firmly encase the whole thing in a layer of chicken wire to form an even surface. The ball will look distinctly amateurish at this stage, but don't worry – flowers will conceal all flaws.

If you are making a 'tree', use a slim wooden dowel, available from timber merchants, or perhaps entwine several thin, leafless branches of beech together and tie them at the top with ribbon or raffia. Whatever upright pole you use, make sure it is heavy enough to balance the height and weight of the ball. Stand the 'trunk' in a clay flowerpot and pack stones or pebbles tightly around it; this will provide weight and rigidity. You can cover the top with soil and a layer of moss for a natural finish, or poke flowers and twigs into the crevices. A bowl is an alternative to the flowerpot, but make sure it is deep enough to be weighted down properly. Push the prepared ball onto the 'trunk', and fix it firmly with wire.

A floral ball containing moist plastic foam and fresh flowers can be very weighty, so hang it up by a length of wire (later concealed by ribbon) attached securely to the chicken wire base. To hang a ball of dried flowers, encircle the plastic foam two or three times with wire or string before you begin, and then suspend the finished ball by ribbon attached to the wire or string at the top.

Start covering the ball with flowers. You will make life easier if you choose flowers with tough, strong stems and tough strong characters – chrysanthemums, carnations and pinks, roses and dahlias. Orchids, a really lavish luxury if you can justify the extravagance, are sensational. Daisies, on the other hand, look superb too – surprisingly fresh, and cost little. A different unexpected delight is the use of daisy-like bright pink flowers or pyrethrum, or any of the single, richly-coloured chrysanthemums such as those opposite. More delicate flowers (like sweet peas) can also be used but you run a great risk of damaging or marking the petals during construction. To stop delicate stems from bending as you insert them, make holes in the foam with an awl or skewer. Spraying the floral ball with a very fine mist will help keep it fresh.

If you want a perfectly smooth ball to become a 'fabric' of flowers (such as carnations packed solidly against each other), make sure all the flower stems are short and of

A well placed mirror doubles the visual value of this chrysanthemum-packed floral ball. As with the dried-flower 'tree' on page 80, plastic foam, roughly cut to a ball shape and wrapped in chicken wire, forms the substructure. If you want the floral ball to last longer than the length of a party, soak the foam first, but drain it thoroughly and put a layer of aluminium foil on the bottom, between the foam and the chicken wire, to catch drips. The ball, when finished, is surprisingly heavy, and the ribbons conceal the wire from which it hangs.

equal length, and push them into the plastic foam as far as they will go. If you want a less formal floral ball, vary both the lengths of the flower stems and the depth to which you push them in, then build up like a painting, flower by flower. Whatever the final effect, gradually increase the

density of the flowers until there is no plastic foam left exposed and you are pleased with the overall result. The basic technique for making a floral ball can be used in so many variations, each a specific response to the room-setting or the occasion.

A FLORAL PALETTE

Though eccentric, perhaps even wrong (some of my friends think so) to start a chapter by mentioning those flowers which I heartily dislike, I do it to make a strong point. Taste in flowers is as personal, subjective and unassailable as taste in clothes, music or paintings. This book is about my own taste (I hope not too far away from yours), and quite naturally extends to the choice of my flower palette. There are many flowers I love, and three I hate, which I shall deal with first – and then move on in greater detail, and with greater pleasure, to the others.

FLORAL FOIBLES

The bird of paradise *(Strelitzia reginae)* tops my floral 'hit list': the one I instinctively think of as 'the hawk'. It has some validity growing wild in the southern hemisphere – and how I wish it could remain there, together with the *Anthuriums,* which I dislike almost as much. With ever increasing volume, though, these flowers have winged their way to other countries and other climates, where they show up in expensive drawing-rooms and hotels. To me, they resemble plastic fairground souvenirs. Ironically, because I dislike them so, they have a way of gravitating towards me – especially when I visit Brazil, where they are always sent to me as a gesture of welcome and hospitality. And many years ago, the *Strelitzia* was somehow inexplicably chosen as my symbolic flower by an American florists' association. If only they had asked me, I'd have suggested a rose or settled just as happily for a daisy.

The gladiolus comes next on my list. Yes, I know it brings brilliant patches of colour to herbaceous borders, and no yacht is considered properly dressed without an oversized vase of gladioli chained to the table, but I do wish they could be kept out of houses. I remember a charity event which I once reluctantly attended. The huge ballroom had been transformed into one stupendous gladiolus, if such a thing is imaginable. Thousands of gladioli had been

An array of summer flower faces makes a mosaic of pure colour. Small, water-filled jars inside the shallow woven basket keep the flowers fresh.

removed from their stalks, and tucked into wire netting which covered the walls, columns and ceiling. At floor level, dark, mahogany-coloured flowers were used, grading up to the palest peach blossom at ceiling level. The effect was that of monstrous gladioli obliterating the original room, and I longed to ask why the obviously enormous and extravagant outlay of money had not been given instead to the charity for which the ball was held.

Another time when gladioli featured perversely is believed to have been after the first gala performance in Paris of the Bolshoi Ballet, at the end of World War II. The evening was as glamorous as war-weary men and women could manage; stage, screen and government luminaries filled the seats. After an exciting performance, immense bouquets, complete with the ever-present gladioli, filled the stage. The Russian dancers reacted as they always do, by sending flowers back to the audience as a gesture of their own appreciation. Pulling the largest flowers from their bouquets (they had to be the gladioli, of course), they hurled them towards the audience – each one becoming a weapon as they whistled past, taking one tiara with them and nearly damaging an eye. The audience either rocked with laughter or shrieked in panic, trying to take avoiding action. It is not for nothing that the gladiolus is commonly called the sword lily.

FLORAL FAVOURITES

Now I move on to my favourite flowers, listed in order of my own personal preferences. This wasn't easy as I love them all, but I finally made my choices. Over the years and in various climates I have used hundreds of different flowers in my arrangements. If you count the many named varieties, these flowers probably number in the thousands rather than the hundreds. In the limited space of one chapter, I couldn't possibly begin to name them all or there would be less information, fewer ideas and reminiscences. Instead, I have picked out some of my most favourite flowers as a personal bouquet. I hope the selection, limited though it is, inspires you to develop favourites of your own. Visit friends' gardens, and garden centres, botanical gardens, flower shows and horticultural shows. Send away for catalogues (even if you don't grow flowers) and never be afraid to try something new.

Damask rose ('Madame Hardy')

Species rose (*Rosa gallica*)

Floribunda rose ('Iceberg')

Rose

It must be no surprise that I begin with the rose *(Rosa)*, the world's (and my) favourite. Roses cross all geographical, financial and social barriers, growing in royal gardens and flourishing just as happily in the large tin cans found hanging from the sunlit, whitewashed cottage walls in southern European countries. Rose gardens are the hobby and pleasure of the great landowners on both sides of the Atlantic, and few suburban gardens are without their show of hybrid tea or floribunda roses. Even during World War II, many British vegetable plots boasted at least one rose bush amid the potatoes and tomatoes.

Roses have been here for 5,000 years, and for much of its long history the rose has been imbued with symbolism. It has sacred, romantic and even historical connotations. The Koran placed it in the Garden of Paradise even before the Garden of Eden. Cleopatra covered the floor with inches of rose petals to seduce Mark Anthony, and Josephine, France's first Empress, gave roses her royal backing by planting them by the thousand in her garden at Malmaison. Her command to Redouté to paint them led to his lasting fame as the greatest of all painters of the rose. Many other painters' love affairs with the rose are recorded in art history, particularly the Dutch Masters, followed by Fantin-Latour, Cézanne, Renoir and numerous others.

Creating rose arrangements is an art, though a transient and small-scale one compared with the works of the great painters. And they aren't always small scale. I once went to extremes to create a rose 'conversation piece' for a dinner party. I started with a huge, square woven basket, sprayed a dark mahogany. I carefully dug up four tall, dark red rose bushes – roots and all – which I then planted inside the lined basket. I next tucked half a dozen of the largest water-filled florist's vials I ever found into the soil between the plants – each one for a tall white cut lily. The result was the essence of an English flower border in full

bloom, and the size of the display was so breathtaking I was genuinely proud of it. A few days later, the lightly watered rose bushes were returned to my garden. I used the idea later in a far more modest way by filling a small basket with one short but plump rose bush in flower, surrounding it by vials filled with such small summer flowers as pinks, geraniums, or coral bells *(Heuchera)*. Once I used only small sprigs of philadelphus.

Another time, I put three short-stemmed pink roses in a water-glass on a table, surrounded by a circle of the same glasses with pale yellow roses. I've also surrounded pink roses with wonderfully coloured yellowy-green lady's mantle, and I pair pink roses with pale green zinnias – using the zinnias as a frame. The idea is equally pleasant, whether in a cup or a large bowl.

I've learned the practical value of planting or buying floribunda roses; their value for money cannot be exaggerated. Because there are so many blooms to a branch, it doesn't take many to make a bouquet, but you can also divide up each short flowering stem to make a number of clusters for small containers.

The cottage rose has always been very popular and is a great friend of flower arrangers. My affection is for their old-fashioned-ness – usually so different from many modern catalogue varieties. The Albas, Bourbons, Damasks and Gallicas belong to the antiquities of the rose garden, the old pre-1900 types. Ask for them; the sight of one in a glass or a dozen in a porcelain or silver jug will make you feel happy.

Flower colours can be used with a painter's eye, and roses probably offer the richest palette. I'm particularly fond of using them in a range of the same colours for a large display: burgundy, crimson, garnet and deep pink roses are a fascinating combination and the newly fashionable apricot and orange colours are another; use them in wine buckets. Harder to find, but worth the effort, are bouquets of different tones of white roses; you can get ones with a greenish, creamy-yellow, or a pink cast – or dead white. In my garden I planted white 'Iceberg' roses against the age-darkened walls of my Sussex barn, and added white pansies and white alyssum to the borders.

Cecil Beaton, Britain's late court photographer, artist and writer, once said of roses, 'White ones are the only chic ones'. I would say they are *among* the most chic, keeping in mind the elegance of long-stemmed roses in deepest red. Neither is 'wrong': such opinions overlap rather than contradict.

In my own garden, I also keep a place for the moss roses I never find in shops. It takes so few to delight the eye. They also appeal to the heart, for they are the particular roses that inspired so many 'antique' valentines. The deep, deep purply-red 'William Lobb', sometimes called 'Old Velvet Moss', is a special favourite.

Tulip

The word 'tulip' comes from the Turkish word 'Tulipan', meaning turban. From Turkey it travelled to France, Austria and, most importantly, to Holland, where it became the object of dizzy speculation. Fortunes were made and lost as 'futures' in bulbs were traded but the 'paper' boom collapsed as quickly as it began. Nevertheless, the world-wide popularity of the tulip *(Tulipa)* as a garden flower never decreased; it is the pet of the poor as well as the rich, and today there are thousands of varieties (with new ones being brought onto the market every year). But as hard as it is to choose, I think I prefer the paeony-flowered tulips and the elusive and elegant 'black' tulip.

The proper name of paeony-flowered tulips is Double Early, and they make a great show in my garden in early and mid-spring. They can also be forced ahead of season, either to use in pots or to make tighly massed bouquets. It is foolish to discuss any flower by colour, the tulip least of all, as it has a remarkable range and even occurs in combinations of colours. If tulip drama is your aim, start with the striped and sometimes fringed parrot tulips. The form 'Fantasy' is pink streaked with green, and 'Black Parrot' is an exquisite, purple-black. And I must mention the 'Viridiflora' tulips, with green shadings on the outer petals. A clump of parrot or viridiflora tulips in a bowl rewards you with new colours every day as they unfold to show their linings. In terms of value for money, plant or buy multiflora tulips because they carry several flowers on each stem.

An interesting tulip trick: turn the petals back upon themselves and the flower becomes almost unrecognizable, in fact much more exotic. The centres are marvellously multicoloured in black, white, red or yellow which when the flower is closed, is a closely guarded secret. Tulips naturally open out as they age – which is in a matter of days – while it would take you a minute or two to turn the petals back. Display these opened-out tulips in a shallow centrepiece or on a low coffee table, so you can look down onto their exquisite faces.

Try cutting the tulip stem just above the leaves. Put the flowers in the centre of a container, then let the leaves hang tightly like a pale green waterfall over the edge of the container.

Try making a circle of tulips, using a different colour for each ring. Or pick out the two dominant colours in a room (look at your wallpaper, curtain and upholstery fabric and carpet) and repeat just those two colours in a leafless, densely packed bunch of tulips.

I like to see tulip stems arched in natural shapes in bowls, rather than in a stiff, upright position. Nature intended them to fall into graceful arches rather than to stand straight up. The arrangement on page 92 shows how, even when their stems are well-supported, tulips will twist and bend into arcs. Tulips grow even after being cut, and should be allowed to do so unhampered.

Double Early tulips

'Black' parrot and Darwin tulips

Lily-flowered tulips

Lily-of-the-valley (*Convallaria majalis*)

Purple-leaved violet (*Viola labradorica* 'Purpurea')

Lily-of-the-Valley

Tiny and tender, the lily-of-the-valley (*Convallaria majalis*) is an old-fashioned favourite (it is the flower I always receive from my husband). France's ancient tradition of celebrating May Day with *muguets* (lilies-of-the-valley) still exists. Children sell bunches of them on the roadsides outside Paris; I can never resist them and their outstretched hands. The French bunch them differently from the way we do: the lilies-of-the-valley are ringed around their tall leaves, like a hat with a feather in the centre. (I now also do this with daffodils.) Lily-of-the-valley corms are expensive but if you can grow them you will be saving money, as they are long-lived perennials and I've never found them inexpensive to buy. A big clump isn't essential; one flower in something as small as an ink-bottle is as beautiful in a room as it was in a Dutch painting I saw in a museum in Amsterdam. If you are as adventurous as I suggest you be with crocuses (and I promise you it will pay off, see page 135), put one lily-of-the-valley, complete with roots, bulb and flowers, in a plain kitchen glass.

Although improving upon the lily-of-the-valley is rather like the proverbial 'gilding the lily', you can grow forms with double flowers, pale pink flowers, or gold-variegated leaves. You are unlikely, however, to find any of these as cut flowers in florists' shops.

Violet

In ancient Greece, the violet was second only to the rose. It was the city flower of Athens, and garlands of violets were worn on fête days. In Greek mythology, the violet was originally white, but when Venus became jealous of Cupid's admiration of the violet's purity she turned the flower from white to deep purple.

Napoleon was called 'Père de la violette', or 'Father of the violet' because of his great love of the flower. When he was exiled to Elba, he said he'd return when violets were in season. Violet ribbons were worn in the hair of women who awaited his return, and brave men hung their watches on violet ribbons as a dangerous, but identifiable, act of patriotism. And when Napoleon did return to Paris again, he found all the paths in the Tuileries covered with fresh violet flowers.

Queen Victoria made the violet fashionable in England. After Prince Albert's death, over 4,000 were planted in Windsor by the sorrowing Queen. Alexandra was another queen who was fond of this small flower, but displayed it very differently – by pinning a small bunch of violets to her muff or to the lapels of her fur coat (two fashions I'd like to see revived).

The violet is a modest flower because of its smallness. Its scent is fragrant but elusive and very short lasting. Though a posy of violets is less bold than a bunch of roses, it is just as romantic.

The violet was Colette's favourite flower. I went to visit her before her death and there by her bedside were four small bunches of this tiny flower. Violets never meant more to me, before or since. I too like a fat bunch of violets in my own home, surrounded by their own leaves and displayed in a tea cup or small glass. The sweet violet (*Viola odorata*) is the violet of my choice, but there are so many other species and varieties – not to mention violas, violettes and pansies, all part of the genus *Viola* – that it is nice to ring the changes from time to time. Even the sweet violet comes in many forms: the blue-violet 'Princess of Wales', the pink 'Coeur d'Alsace' and the double-flowered mauve 'Duchesse du Parme'. These, I'm afraid, you'll have to grow in your own garden, as they are rarely, if ever, available as florists' flowers. Also worth planting in your garden is the lovely purple-leaved violet, *Viola labradorica* 'Purpurea'. A sprawling, slightly sloppy plant, it seeds itself freely and weaves its way through other plants, giving a border or bed a lush, well-knit appearance. The flowers are small and unscented, but charming nevertheless.

Orchid

The orchid is the exact opposite of the violet in imagery, symbolism and implication – considered the caviar of flowers, madly expensive, exotic, rare, flamboyant and even snobbish (though nowadays rather less so). There was a time when only a certain (and to me unacceptable) orchid would do. It was huge and purple, came in a plastic box and was obligatory as a corsage for formal occasions, whether pinned to the bosom or the shoulder – especially on those of dowagers, to whom appearing publicly without one was considered bad form! Fortunately, this sight is rare today.

The least expensive of all orchids are the tiny vanda orchids from Malaysia. They are available now in major chain stores and in just about every florist and are actually a bargain, because of their longevity. A spray of even the most rare, costly orchids will last for several weeks, many times longer than say, the inexpensive daffodil or tulip. The plants (if you have a greenhouse to nourish them later) could flower for months in your house and now are becoming far easier to cultivate.

There are thousands of species and cultivars of orchids, now grown and bred commercially, although in the wild they are almost at the top of the World Wildlife Fund's Endangered Species List. The most commonly available varieties are the cymbidium, the slipper orchids (*Cypripedium* and *Paphiopedilum*) and the odontoglossum. Difficult to get hold of (and grow), yet the one I love the most, is the moth orchid (*Phalaenopsis*) which has a long, slender, gently bending stem ending in the purest of white flowers.

Never embellish an orchid: that is my one unflinching rule. They are usually wasted with other flowers. If I find one included in a gift arrangement, I always remove it to a small vase of its own. It will outlive as well as out-shine all the other flowers of the original arrangement. Orchids are so long lived

that they will even stay crisp and fresh for hours out of water. I have seen sprays of orchids displayed on a beautiful, polished mahogany dining-table during a meal. Replaced in water afterwards, no damage was done.

Paeony

To the Chinese people, the word 'paeony' means 'most beautiful' (and often this means the white ones). Like Cecil Beaton's pronouncement on the supremacy of the white rose, this opinion is mildly controversial, but few would dispute the paeony's intrusive beauty. It, like the tulip, was once sold for gold, as much as 2.7 kilos (199 ounces) for one plant! Some still growing in Peking's Imperial Gardens are two centuries old; the tree paeony has graced Chinese art for many more centuries. The Greeks called it 'paean', after the physician to the Gods who used the roots of this plant to cure their wounds.

The romantic beauty of a bowl of open, pink paeonies cheek-to-cheek is a sight hard to beat. There are other stunning arrangements; try one fat bloom to a brandy glass – a group of six can make a circular centrepiece for a table. Or one short stem and leaf to each glass can march down a table. To me, paeonies mixed with lilacs, whatever the colours, are almost as feminine as a big bowl of mixed garden roses. Cut short for a shallow round bowl and placed on a coffee table, they are wonderful to look down upon.

Although the huge, heavy flowers of tree paeonies (*Paeonia delavayi* with golden-centred, dark red blooms, *Paeonia lutea*, with cup-shaped yellow flowers, and *Paeonia suffruticosa* in many varieties), don't last long, I can never resist cutting them. I pack them tightly in shallow bowls, or set them in brandy glasses on a table as I do with ordinary paeonies. Sometimes I cut them short and cram them into a large round bowl until they almost overflow.

Herbaceous paeonies, on the other hand, can and will stand straight and tall.

Slipper orchid (*Paphiopedilum* species)

Paeony (*Paeonia officinalis* 'Rosea Plena')

Paeony (*Paeonia lactiflora* 'Karl Rosenfeld')

Sweet pea (*Lathyrus odoratus*)

Oriental poppy (*Papaver orientalis*)

Himalayan blue poppy
(*Meconopsis betonicifolia*)

The dark pink forms, such as the single-flowered 'Beersheba' or the fully double 'Edulis Supreme', make lovely companions for purple lilac. Try the deep crimson or ruby-red ones with matching roses for an intensely rich display, or perhaps use the fragile-looking whites such as 'White Wings' and 'Wrinkled White'. The golden-centred single paeonies have fabric-like, crêpe petals.

In your garden, once a paeony takes hold (and that may be years, so be patient), it will last long enough to delight many future generations.

Sweet pea

Sweet peas (*Lathyrus odoratus*) were the first flower seeds I was given as a child, and I have loved them ever since. Sweet peas don't really need companions or adornment. Simple displays of thickly massed flowers, all cut to the same height, are lovely. If you grow sweet peas in your garden, try to include a few of the old-fashioned 'Grandiflora' strain, which has smaller and far less showy flowers than the newer, full 'Spencer' and 'Galaxy' type sweet peas, but has a heavenly fragrance, many times more intense. One or two old-fashioned sweet peas will lift the scent of a whole bowl of modern ones.

Another, relatively recent, development is dwarf sweet peas, which grow like cushions at your feet. Some, like 'Little Sweetheart', have small flowers, while others, such as 'Jet Set', have flowers equal in size and number to the taller-growing types. They are perfect for small gardens; the 'Patio' strain can even be planted in window boxes and hanging baskets, making a fragrant, colourful cascade. I've seen and admired some in the ubiquitous window boxes of London.

Poppy

I love to paint the exquisite, black-centred, white oriental poppy (*Papaver orientale*), which has a mysterious hint of pale green. There are also poppies in shades of raspberry pink,

brilliant orange, brick red, lilac, salmon, scarlet and deep maroon. There are single and double forms of this perennial garden plant, some with fringed or ruffled petals. The opium poppy (*Papaver somniferum*) is an annual, with huge flowers. The opium and heroin obtained from its sap makes it illegal to grow in some hot countries. A most unexpected colour to find in poppies is pure, clear blue, but the Himalayan blue poppy (*Meconopsis betonicifolia*) is just that. A group of them grows in London's Kew Gardens, on the edge of light woodland, and in early summer the shocking clarity of their blueness brings a joy to visitors. The little yellow Welsh poppy (*Meconopsis cambrica*) is a cheerful and modest flower, as easy to grow as the Himalayan poppy is difficult.

Finally, consider the California tree poppy (*Romneya coulteri*). Not a tree at all but halfway between a shrub and a herbaceous perennial, the California tree poppy produces large yellow-centred pure white flowers, with petals in an exaggerated consistency of crêpe. Because it looks like one it is sometimes called the fried egg poppy, and is also called the Matilija poppy.

There is no denying that all of these poppies have short-lived flowers but there is a rescue operation: burn the stem with a candle or match as you pick it. You can then enjoy their comparatively short lives to the fullest. Display them in a loose bouquet in plain glass containers to look as if they're growing, never, never arranged formally.

Lilac

There is nothing nice to be said about lilac leaves. Besides being dull, they rob cut flowers of much-needed water. Indeed, all should be removed as part of the conditioning of each cut stem. The flowers themselves are so wonderful, so necessary for flower lovers, that no garden should be without them. The ordinary lilac (*Syringa vulgaris*) has given its name to a colour, but there are other colours which range from pure white,

Lilac (*Syringa vulgaris* 'Firmament')

Camellia (*Camellia japonica* 'Mathotiana Alba')

yellow, pink, pale blue and red to deepest purple. Lilac doesn't have a long flowering season, so use them extravagantly while they are around. (Fortunately, forced lilac is available from florists in early spring, though the choice of colours is limited.) Surround pink lilacs with deep purple tulips. Combine 'lilac' lilacs with dark red roses, or combine dark red lilacs with the fabulous, lilac-coloured hybrid tea rose, 'Blue Moon'.

Camellia

The camellia is not only an evergreen but also does us the favour of flowering when other plants do not. The flowers came to the West by accident in the late eighteenth century when traders thought, from their scent, they were the flowers of the fashionable tea plants (tea and camellia both belong to the same family *Theaceae*). From this initial error, the Old World and its gardens have benefited.

Remember that while camellias are loved for their flowers, and quite rightly, the value of their leaves shouldn't be overlooked as a result. Their dark green surfaces have such a sheen that they look polished. Try using the leaves on the table to surround the bowl in which you've floated one or more camellia heads.

The pink and red camellias are stunning, but if I could grow or buy only one, I'd grow the pure white *Camellia japonica* 'Alba Simplex'. Its single flowers are admittedly less showy than the semi-double, double, anemone- and paeony-flowered forms, but its purity and elegance is dear to my heart. The shrubs, by the way, are much tougher than was originally thought: they not only grow out of doors but even in shade and in the polluted atmosphere of town gardens, although their flowers can be disfigured and browned by exposure to hard frost. I grow my camellias in tubs and, if frost threatens, take them inside or to the greenhouse. The camellia's only shortcoming, in my view, is that it holds on to its old and spent flowers instead of shedding them to make room for the new. This is particularly unfortunate with white-flowered camellias, which look soiled and dirty when they die. (Lilacs, too, suffer from this problem.) Just a few camellias are glorious on their own in low cups or tucked (where they plainly show) in mixed bouquets. They have the unfailing habit of arranging themselves so just put them gently in water and let them find their own way. One camellia flower head floating in a shallow bowl is a perfect centrepiece for a table set for two, or you could float one in a brandy glass for each place setting.

Camellia (*Camellia × williamsii* 'Donation')

Anemones (*Anemone coronaria* De Caen)

Delphiniums (*Delphinium* hybrids)

Clematis (*Clematis* 'Ville de Lyon')

Anemone

Anemones look like stained glass. Flower painters would be lost without them, and so would we. It hurts me to see them stretching loosely in a bowl; they need huddling together. I sometimes mass just one colour – blue, royal purple, all-white (some have white centres, some have yellow) or, best of all (if your colour scheme allows), fire-engine red. Whether this way or mixed, their impact, on canvas and in real life, is indisputable.

Delphinium

Delphiniums are also called larkspur, and they rank among the most noble of all summer flowers (what would an English border be without them?). On page 22, you'll see how I stole the tallest ones from my garden to use in an umbrella stand – but they are beautiful in any tall container, especially on the floor near a window, or placed to give a bare corner some drama. Where blue is the colour needed, delphiniums give it to you on a theatrical scale but they are equally breathtaking in the pink and white varieties.

Clematis

The clematis, often called Virgin's Bower, was one of the first floral delights to catch my eye when I came to live in England. The sight of the bright pink or lavender clematis climbing over cottages (thatched or otherwise), Georgian doorways, trellises, and trailing over rockwork, ornamental garden urns and greenhouses made me want to have my own country house to put the ubiquitous climber to work. It now forms a long archway over a path – a lovely sight as one comes down the drive to our house. Best of all, I now plant and train it to ramble over fruit trees, as it blooms when their own blossoms are over.

Pansy

Pansies (various *Viola*) are nature's perfect faces: flowers that cry out to be observed and enjoyed at close range (although they are too seldom used

Pansies (*Viola gracilis*)

indoors, perhaps because they aren't easily available from any florist). Their stems can sometimes be too short in relation to the size of the flowers, but this is no handicap if you display them as 'faces'. The photograph on page 27 shows such an arrangement: circles of yellow and red pansies, still discernible as individual flowers but making a visual statement larger than the sum of its parts.

In the garden, I use pale blue pansies to outline two separate borders of salmon pink 'Elizabeth of Glamis' roses, and I do the same when I use both for indoor arrangements, cutting short stems from these floribundas, and adding pansies as a border. You can also try massing pansies into a ball by cutting the stems in graduated lengths. Start with white flowers in the centre, and end with a pale blue flowered border. As a variation on the theme, try pure white pansies with an edging of forget-me-nots or rich blue cornflowers.

It is certainly worth growing some of the winter-flowering pansies, such as 'Floral Dance Mixed', which start flowering in autumn and continue through winter and into spring. If you are as mesmerized by 'black' flowers as I am, grow 'Bowles Black', pansies of such a deep, dark midnight blue colouring that they are very nearly black. Given rich soil and cool, moist root conditions, 'Bowles Black' will seed itself freely in your garden to provide nearly-black flowers for years to come.

Pansies (*Viola* × *wittrockiana* hybrid)

Hyacinth

It seems wantonly destructive to cut the forced flowers of hyacinths *(Hyacinthus)* from their bulbs as the plants look so pretty in groups of single colours and fill a room with scent for weeks on end. But towards the end of their flowering period, the stalks do get a bit leggy and I feel courageous enough to cut them. If I cut more than one I try to group the hyacinths in mixed colours, especially since the pastels on their own can look insipid in a room with strong or vivid colours. Hyacinths, like tulips, have an inclination to arch and curve gracefully, rather than remain poker-straight, and I like to allow them this privilege.

The tiny grape hyacinths *(Muscari)* lack the scent of their larger, more flamboyant cousins, but their tightly packed heads of blue bell-like flowers do say 'Spring is here'. Use grape hyacinths in posies with the primroses, lilies-of-the-valley, early tulips and alyssum that share their flowering period. Or use them alone – perhaps packed tightly into a single glass.

The bluebells *(Endymion non-scriptus)* that grow wild in English woodlands are sometimes called wild hyacinths (both are members of the *Liliaceae* family). Though breeders have developed large-flowered, stiff-stemmed, cultivated forms of bluebell, in white, pink and deep violet as well as blue, it is the wild ones that I love so much – perhaps because I have a large field carpeted in wild ones outside my home. When

picking bluebells cut the stem where it is green, leaving the white section attached to the bulb. This provides nourishment to the bulb, which needs this energy to produce next year's flowers. Bluebells, being informal and modest by nature, should be presented as such. A pale blue tumbler full of water, or a suitable plain vase, is most appropriate.

Nasturtium

This is one annual I never find too much trouble to grow from seed, especially as so few florists stock them. Nasturtiums *(Tropaeolum)* look audacious when mixed in their own bold colours: red, yellow, orange and cream. Remember that the more you pick, the more they flower – so pick them daily and add to the bouquet. There is a small-growing strain, 'Tom Thumb', which I plant along my hedgerows.

Indoors, as cut flowers, they are especially endearing and unpretentious. My ideal container is a gleaming copper pan or a basin or even an enamelled frying-pan – any of which reflect their glorious colours (use their pretty, round, grey-green leaves as a ruffle hanging over the edges). A different idea is to display long trailing stems in a large bowl, with some flowers in bud, others fully opened, and some seed pods. A big clump of nasturtiums isn't essential, however. A single flower and its leaf in an old-fashioned ink pot can play a starring role on a desk or bedside table.

Gypsophila

Baby's breath, the common name, accurately describes its delicacy. It is not beloved for nothing (perhaps only cow parsley can compete with its popularity). Unfortunately, it is often dismissed as a 'filler' flower. A sprig of baby's breath *(Gypsophila paniculata)* is usually automatically included by florists in a bunch of mixed flowers, and as such, its own beauty gets quite lost in the general muddle. Give baby's breath a definite role. Let it be the core of an arrangement; even better, let it be a

Grape hyacinths (*Muscari latifolium*)

Nasturtiums (*Tropaeolum majus*)

Gypsophila (*Gypsophila paniculata* 'Rosy Veil')

generous, lace-like hem. Unusual? Yes, but effective because unexpected. Baby's breath is even beautiful unattended by other flowers. Did you know that, besides white ones, there are pale pink flowered varieties too: 'Flamingo', 'Pink Star' and 'Rosy Veil'? I've yet to come across these, but am determined, sooner or later, to do so.

Daffodil

In England, some spring gardens are entirely given over to daffodils; tourists often come to the cities to visit the parks which display daffodils like vast yellow and white carpets. But even these large-scale municipal displays pale in comparison with the daffodils of Sutton Place. The grounds surrounding this Tudor mansion which once belonged to the late Paul Getty, display many, many thousands of daffodils, a thrilling sight well worth the short journey from London (Sutton Place, near Guildford in Surrey, is open by appointment).

Don't try to gild the lily when it comes to arranging daffodils *(Narcissus)* indoors. Simply mass them in a container as nearly like a great ball of colour as you can make them. When they are in season, and genuinely inexpensive, repeat daffodil arrangements in room after room after room and you'll bring spring indoors!

Present daffodils as if they were growing. Half-fill a clear glass container with earth. Add water nearly up to the brim and leave it to settle for an hour. When the earth drops to the bottom of the container (with clean, clear water at the top), gently pack the container with daffodils, so that their stems rest in the earth. This idea works just as well with the heavenly-scented 'Paper White' narcissi as it does with the common daffodil. You can, if you like, include a few leaves for an even more natural effect. Using a huge shallow glass dish or copper pan, try mixing tiny snowdrops, violets or primroses in the same 'growing' display by cutting the stems all the same length.

Scabious

Among the few blue flowers easily available in summer (the cornflower, delphinium, pansy and forget-me-not among them), the perennial scabious *(Scabiosa caucasica)* is high on my list, especially the ruffled ones I buy from my florist. The plants produce very few flowers at a time (though the flowering season is itself quite long). The common name, 'pincushion flower', comes from

Daffodils (*Narcissus* 'February Gold')

Annual scabious (*Scabiosa atropurpurea*)

Pinks (*Dianthus chinensis*)

the fact that the bristle-packed central disc of the flower looks like one; it is surrounded by pale blue, paper-thin petals. As with cornflower, the plant breeders have come up with scabious in other colours, but the blue remains most generally useful.

The annual sweet scabious *(Scabiosa atropurpurea)* has a luscious deep maroon (almost black) form among the white, pink, blue, red and mauve flowers obtained from a packet of mixed seed. It is a pity that packets of seed of just that dark, rich colour alone aren't available. Scabious and baby's breath are a fresh and summery combination. Or put a few short-stemmed scabious in each of several containers, such as the tiny Victorian Parian containers shown on page 35 which used comparatively few flowers. In fact one or two bunches went a long, long way.

Incidentally, the flat pale green unopened buds of scabious are as pretty as the opened flowers, and should be included in your bouquet. The long-lasting pretty seed pods that remain after the petals have fallen are a further bonus.

Carnation

The French Riviera's hillsides are covered with carnations. I remember particularly the late couturier Captain Edward Molyneux's commercial carnation farm there, which he designed as a series of dipping terraces. It was a delight to sit on his patio overlooking the hillsides, looking down on the waterfall of these flowers. Absorbing the beauty and fragrance of those carnations was an unforgettable experience. Because they are moderately priced and available all year round, I sometimes feel that carnations *(Dianthus)* are taken for granted and used without much thought.

A pet hate I share with many friends is the dyed carnation. The chemical colours look unpleasantly unnatural: a forlorn bunch of mixed dyed carnations with a lonely sprig of baby's breath or asparagus fern may be, for me, the worst possible floral twosome. But a large bouquet of carnations (no foliage, please) in every natural conceivable colour can't be faulted. Soon the stems will twist and turn slightly, mixing the colours even more. There are few more practical everyday flowers.

Use carnations tightly packed together in hanging floral balls, in high-rise balls on dowels or as a simple high-rise table display (as on page 21). Though these large, perpetual-flowering carnations are excellent for providing a mass of colour, small border carnations and garden pinks have far more charm. There is an enormous range of old-fashioned and modern ones with scented, single or double flowers in marvellous colours and colour combinations. Some have contrasting flecks, stripes or edging, with a contrasting central colour and even 'lacing' of a second colour over white, yellow, pink, salmon, crimson, scarlet, mauve, maroon and bright cerise petals. Really, the best source of these lovely flowers has to be your own garden, and you may need to find a specialist nursery to obtain the plants.

Sweet William *(Dianthus barbatus)* is a modest, biennial, cottage-garden cousin of carnations – luckily, one as easy to grow as to buy. Each flat head is tightly packed with open-faced flowers, and putting them together, head to head, creates an incredibly rich effect. Cut the stems to the same length (try them short rather than mixed lengths if you want a change); the flowers will become an uninterrupted tapestry of colour. Besides being inexpensive, sweet Williams last, last, last. Try surrounding a short-stemmed mass of dark red and maroon sweet Williams with the equally long-lasting white stars of Bethlehem *(Ornithogalum umbellatum)*. The outer ring becomes an unexpected white 'ruffle' for the wild range of colours of sweet Williams. Or start with a central core of pale pink sweet Williams, surrounding it with concentric circles of gradually deepening colours, ending with a circle of deep, wine red.

Cornflower
Though there are perennial cornflowers, it is the annual form *(Centaurea cyanus)* that is most useful for my purposes. Inexpensive and blue (a rare combination), cornflowers look lovely surrounding a central core of cow parsley (Queen Anne's lace), all stems having been cut to the same length; for a very small outlay, you end up with quite a large bouquet. Besides the well known bright blue cornflower, there are now white, pink, purple and red forms, but my loyalty is to the blue.

Crocus
The crocus is a transplant from the wild. The little lavender *(Crocus tomasinianus)* is one of our earliest bloomers, emerging as early as January and waiting patiently for a few sunny days to open the flower. I always dig up a dozen bulbs at this stage to replant in the oblong, lined, narrow basket I keep for the purpose; there are

Crocus (*Crocus tomasinianus*)

few more endearing sights. The bulbs eventually go back in the ground. Perhaps your florist will make you such a basket arrangement.

Lily
My most memorable view of lilies was when I visited the late flower expert Beverley Nichols. His London house was ablaze with countless bunches of beautiful white regal lilies *(Lilium regale),* their scent almost overpowering. In the garden which surrounded his Georgian house were hundreds more, growing with the exuberance and vigour of wild flowers. When questioned, he said that regal lilies were extremely easy to grow and I have learned, to my delight, how right he was. Given well-drained, decent soil and full sun, they increase rapidly and will soon supply enough for cutting as well as for

Sweet Williams (*Dianthus barbatus*)

Cornflowers (*Centaurea cyanus*)

Madonna lily (*Lilium candidum*)

Arum lily (*Zantedeschia aethiopica*)

African lily (*Agapanthus* 'Headbourne Hybrid')

the garden. The madonna lily *(Lilium candidum)* is pure white and flawless, appearing in our gardens early. Among the most spectacular are the tiger lilies *(Lilium tigrinum)*, with their orange and black jungle-like markings. Other lilies come in any colour except true blue. A single stem of lilies, or even one flower, needs no apology or accompaniment.

A word of advice: lily pollen can stain the flowers yellow (also your fingers and clothes), and commercial growers often remove the pollen-carrying anthers before sending lilies to market. If this hasn't been done, or if you are cutting lilies from your garden, quickly remove the orange anthers. Lilies, like orchids, are not cheap to buy but, like orchids, are very good value for money as they last and last and last.

There are many flowers that don't belong to the genus *Lilium* but have, one way or another, acquired the name 'lily'. One is the austere, even funereal, arum lily *(Zantedeschia aethiopica)* with its odd, finger-like central yellow spadix and surrounding white, flower-like spathe. I have a mania for the African lily *(Agapanthus)* with its crowded heads of trumpet-shaped, clear blue flowers, and use them to outline the walls of my home in Spain. If you are growing them, I recommend the 'Headbourne Hybrids' which are generally considered the hardiest. Use African lilies alone on their long, graceful and leafless stems, or remove the stems to observe their tiny faces close up in low containers.

Looking rather like a pink version of the African lily is the Guernsey lily *(Nerine sarniensis)*. If you haven't got a greenhouse or a very sheltered garden, grow *Nerine bowdenii* instead. The best thing about nerines (aside from their most glorious colours) is the late season when they are in flower – from September to November. While the garden becomes less and less flowered, nerines bloom in great profusion and seem to last interminably when cut.

The day lily *(Hemerocallis)*, as its name suggests, has flowers that last for one day

Foxtail lily (*Eremurus robustus*)

only. Still, if you have a clump of day lilies in your garden, flowers continue to be produced over many weeks, and flowers for daily replacement are always to hand. There are some insipid pale orange forms, but there are also some staggeringly beautiful named forms which include 'Morocco Red' (a yellow-centred maroon form), and the deep pink 'Pink Prelude'. Don't lament their short lives; enjoy them to the fullest.

The foxtail lily *(Eremurus)* and giant lily *(Cardiocrinum giganteum)* are both enormous, suitable for large-scale displays demanding flowers as high as 8m (6ft) tall! They are not easy to come by, either in florists' shops or in garden centres, so a specialist nursery is likely to be your only source. Also rare, but definitely not giant, is the glory lily *(Gloriosa)*, with exotic, turk's-cap-shaped flowers, in a combination of red, yellow and black. Rather like a passionflower in the intricacy of its construction, one glory lily blossom in a water-filled finger-bowl will captivate both the eye and the conversation.

The Peruvian lily *(Alstroemeria)*, particularly the 'Ligtu Hybrids' form, is altogether more accessible from the florist or garden centre. Once established in your garden, it tends to

Peruvian lilies (*Alstroemeria aurantiaca*)

take over from weaker neighbours and you may find that you have more than you think you want. Still, you can never have too many of their trumpet-shaped flowers, which can be white, yellow, pink, orange, salmon or scarlet, striped and spotted with contrasting colours. Let them take over your house when they are most profuse in the garden.

Iris

Irises come in so many colours, from white to near black, creams, yellows, pinks, mauves, purples, all the blues and even green, that I sometimes wish I could devote my whole garden to them – an extremely expensive desire! Though the tall bearded varieties are those most often seen in gardens (flowering in late spring and early summer), there are dozens more to try. In the depths of winter, for example, the tiny *Iris reticulata* is in flower by my door in the country – and so is the exquisite Algerian iris *(Iris unguicularis)*. The latter, in fact, sometimes starts flowering in late autumn and continues on and off as winter permits, through early spring. You won't find these at the florist's as they are short-lived once cut, but if you have the room they are certainly worth growing. The rhizomes of irises can be cut and divided every couple of years. Only the younger, outer sections should be used, and the older, central portion discarded. The tall upright stems of *Iris pallida* hybrids make unusual cut flowers

(few people cut their garden irises – I'll never know why) and they will bring their mysterious and exquisite scent to the room.

The irises available from florists are usually the Dutch, English and Spanish forms *(Iris xiphium* hybrids), shorter than the bearded garden irises and in a more limited colour range. These are the ones I used in the arrangement on page 95; by massing the individual flowers into a solid block of colour, a very exotic and rarified effect is created. One commercially available iris that needs no help in looking exotic is the snake's head iris *(Hermodactylus tuberosus)*, with small flowers of green and velvety black. These are cold, jewel-like flowers, best used in an all-white setting.

Chrysanthemum

As with dahlias, I am afraid that huge, grapefruit-sized blooms leave me cold – or relatively cold, compared to the much smaller, single, daisy-like chrysanthemums, such as those used in the floral ball on page 123. If I'm sent a big bunch of the large-flowered chrysanthemums, I always rearrange them. Sometimes I cut the flower heads off and float them, singly or massed (in single colours) in shallow containers. Other times I tie a few heads very tightly together to make one *really* huge one – so 'unreal' it is beautiful! I've seen large, pale pink bouquets in an all-white room and had to admit that they were a fabulous sight, but a huge display of already-huge chrysanthemums in a small room doesn't really work (too reminiscent of outsized floral displays in hotel corridors).

The first spider chrysanthemums I saw at the Chelsea Flower Show years ago were a shock, but I soon grew accustomed to them and eventually began to enjoy using them. White spider chrysanthemums with their curved petals lack the flatness of white ordinary chrysanthemums, which I sometimes think should be reserved for weddings and wedding receptions only.

Iris (*Iris stylosa*)

Spider chrysanthemums
(*Chrysanthemum* 'White Spider')

Semi-pompon chrysanthemums
(*Chrysanthemum* 'Hunstanton')

Forget-me-nots (*Myosotis alpestris*)

Summer jasmine (*Jasminum officinale*)

Schizanthus (*Schizanthus* 'Monarch Strain')

Forget-me-not

Although they are sold as bedding plants, I ignore this fact and recommend you to ask your florist to get the long-lasting little forget-me-nots *(Myosotis)* for you to make into tiny blue bouquets on their own, or as an edge to other small flowers to enlarge a bouquet.

Jasmine

Summer jasmine *(Jasminum officinale)* climbs walls and brings fragrance to rooms above ground, or, if not trained against a wall, it develops into low, fat shrub which, in season, become a mass of tiny white flower clusters, filling the garden with a heavy fragrance which matches the beauty of the flowers. I cut short strands to wind in and around roses; I also mix them with short spikes of lavender (how they scent the room!) or I use them in exactly the same way as I do clematis.

Schizanthus

This is a flower I prefer to use potted. It is often called the butterfly flower, and its contrastingly blotched brightly coloured flowers are available from summer through to autumn. Its other common name is poor man's orchid, because of the dozens of miniature orchid-like blooms on each stem. Group two or three pots together in a large container for the best effect.

Rhododendron

If you have the space and time to grow rhododendrons (most are very slow growing) they will doubly reward you with long-lasting, shiny green leaves as well as flowers. Once cut, the flowers are relatively short lived, but they produce a dramatic sight. Sometimes their crooked stems may refuse to behave the way I want them to when I'm arranging a large display. If this happens, I snip off any unwieldy lower stems and float their heads in a water-filled plate as a centrepiece. Another solution is to construct a pure block of colour from the tightly packed flowers, formal and

Rhododendron (*Rhododendron* hybrid)

geometric, leafless rather than leafy. Incidentally, this works equally well with oversized dahlias and chrysanthemums.

Dahlia

Though I cannot say I love the dahlia, I cannot ignore it in its many forms for flower arranging. Perhaps my least favourites are the dahlias whose sole *raison d'être* is their hugeness. I prefer the small, pompon dahlias, which retain the glowing colours of their larger relatives without their ungainly size. In the arrangement on page 8, I have used vivid red dahlias in the middle-sized range. As you can see, they are so exciting on their own that they need no embellishment. I removed their leaves, as much to extend the life of the flowers as to concentrate on the flower alone: dahlia leaves are particularly thirsty, and cause the premature wilting of the flower. Dahlias always look best tightly packed rather than standing awkwardly as sentinels on their poker-straight stalks. If I feel that foliage is necessary, I still pack the heads tightly together and then insert into the bouquet sprigs of other leaves less greedy than those of the dahlia. Softly coloured larch is one

Pompon dahlia (*Dahlia* 'Kay Helen')

alternative, and so are the brightly splashed and speckled coleus leaves if the colours match. I also try cutting all dahlia stems to exactly the same length and using them tightly packed in a soup tureen as a table centrepiece. Instead of dahlias of one colour only, you may prefer a brightly chaotic mix of many colours. Another possibility with mixed colours is to fill several small shallow bowls with short-stemmed dahlias, each in a different colour, then put the bowls together in a circle; from above you see a composite mosaic. By the way, the dahlia was originally grown in its native Mexico for the roots, which were eaten as food, and not for the flowers.

Daisy – and daisy-like flowers
Last (because of its multitudinous varieties), but not least, is the daisy. I can never have too many. Their open, friendly and uncomplicated faces have given me years of delight, and I've used them in many guises. Ending this chapter with my cherished daisy seems appropriate.

One of the most beautiful bridal bouquets that I have ever seen was composed of long-stemmed Shasta daisies (*Chrysanthemum maximum*) tied with a

wide white satin ribbon. The bride's dress, in pure white organdie, was the perfect foil, and proved, yet again, that the innocence of this bouquet was just right for a very young and beautiful girl. At Grace Kelly's marriage to Prince Rainier, all the little flower-girls carried tiny posies of daisies.

Daisy-like flowers come in numerous magical varieties: the moon daisy (*Chrysanthemum uliginosum*) is quite ordinary-looking except for its incredible height. Reaching 1.8m (6ft), the tall stems make it perfect for high-rise arrangements. There are some lovely annual chrysanthemums that provide yellow, white or multicolour 'daisies' in the summer months. *Chrysanthemum carinatum* is commonly called the tricolour chrysanthemum, a name which accurately describes the rings, bands and zones of crimson, yellow, bronze, red and white on the petals, which surround the deep purple centre. More traditionally daisy-like in colour is *Chrysanthemum coronarium* with white, yellow-edged white or pure yellow daisy flowers.

The Barberton daisy *(Gerbera jamesonii)* has become much more widely grown in recent years, and consequently less expensive. These are in masses of colours and I find the pale apricot forms and the palest dusky pink ones absolutely irresistible. As with freesias, I don't like to see Barberton daisies arranged, and, again as with freesias, they also make a vivid impression in mixed colours. However, a more austere, sophisticated and modern impression can be achieved with one colour only. Try tucking the flowers (with a florist's vial attached to each stem) into a centrepiece made of a mound of lemons and oranges.

Both the Barberton daisy and the African daisy *(Arctotis)* are native to South Africa. If you want to use these intensely coloured flowers, you'll enjoy growing your own (in full sun or the flowers will simply refuse to open). A packet of mixed seeds of *Arctotis hybrida* will give you flowers in every shade of yellow, cream, red, orange, salmon and

Shasta daisies (*Chrysanthemum maximum*)

Barberton daisies (*Gerbera jamesonii*)

African daisy (*Arctotis grandis*)

European daisy (*Bellis perennis*)

Rudbeckia hirta 'Marmalade'

Sunflower (*Helianthus annuus* 'Sunburst')

apricot, and some of the flowers will be two-toned. My favourite is the blue-eyed African daisy *(Arctotis grandis),* a pure white flower with a deep blue centre, rimmed in palest gold. Always pick African daisies when the flowers are fully open, and place them in a sunny spot indoors. They close at night, but should open again in the morning, if they're given plenty of sunlight.

A blue daisy is almost too much to hope for, but the little Swan River daisy *(Brachycome iberidifolia)* and the kingfisher daisy *(Felicia bergeriana)* are just that. The former is black-eyed, and the latter has centres of bright yellow, but both are half-hardy annuals which you'll have to grow yourself if you want them for cutting. I think they look best in tight bouquets, without embellishment or competition from other flowers.

The tiny European, or English, daisy *(Bellis perennis)* is, for some reason, a most unwelcome weed when it shows up in lawns (other than in mine, where I love them). On the other hand, they have given countless hours of summer pleasure to children, who join them together to make daisy chains and bracelets, necklaces and fairy-tale circlets for their hair. This is probably the best use to make of them, but some of their larger, cultivated cousins can be used in small-scale bouquets in late spring and summer. The double-flowered forms look just like buttons, in shades of red, pink or white. Tuck either these or the large single-flowered forms into beds of moss in a shallow container or make small nosegays in tiny vases.

Michaelmas daisies *(Aster novi-belgii)* light up the garden in autumn, and can light up your home as well. They don't mix socially with other flowers, and don't take to being dressed up formally. Pick as many as you can and plonk them into a simple container in a haze of purple, pink, white, mauve or violet blue.

The glorious daisy *(Rudbeckia hirta* variety) is like an extra-large black-eyed Susan, with flowers up to 17cm (7in) across. There are semi-double and

double forms, but it is the single ones that are most daisy-like in character, which I prefer. Those named 'Irish Eyed' have unusual, green-centred flowers with bright yellow petals.

The giants of all the daisies are sunflowers *(Helianthus annuus).* Their common name gives no indication that they, like daisies, belong to the Compositae family except for the absolute evidence of their daisy-flower faces. These are the flowers that Van Gogh twisted and contorted in his paintings, prints of which have sold by the million all over the world and are viewed as a source of pleasure, not a record of Van Gogh's private mental pain. Sunflowers are now recognized internationally as an emblem of his work. The real flowers are even more popular, and are especially beloved by young children.

Sunflowers are the ideal 'starter' plant for new gardeners of whatever age – they are so easy to cultivate (and you can watch them grow). An English custom of which I am particularly fond is the sponsorship of children's sunflowers for charity. As a sponsor, you agree (before the seed is sown) to give a certain amount to a named charity for every 2.5cm (1in) in height to which the stem grows. The child then has the double thrill of nurturing and observing the growing plant, while raising money for a worthy cause as it grows.

The largest sunflowers include the form 'Russian Giant', which grows to a height of 3m (10ft). They are suitable indoors only for spectacular high-rise displays in umbrella stands or in heavy large containers for the floor in corners of rooms – or as stemless faces to be seen at very close range. The smaller forms – smaller both in height and flower size – combine beautifully with the foliage of late summer and early autumn. Try the yellow, red and mahogany flowers of 'Autumn Beauty' with the blue-black berries of elder or the wine-purple foliage of smoke trees *(Cotinus coggygria* 'Royal Purple').

SPECIALLY PROTECTED WILD PLANTS

The following British plants are protected by the Wildlife and Countryside Act, 1981, and it is against the law to pick, remove or sell these plants or any parts of them, or to collect or sell their seed. It is also illegal to dig up, without the consent of the owner or occupier, any wild plant. This list may be updated from time to time, as new plants are threatened with extinction or protected plants become less rare. If you are in doubt about a particular plant, check with the Nature Conservancy Council or the Botanical Society of the British Isles, c/o Department of Botany British Museum (Natural History).

Adder's-tongue spearwort
  Ranunculus ophioglossifolius
Alpine catchfly
  Lychnis alpina
Alpine gentian
  Gentiana nivalis
Alpine sow-thistle
  Cicerbita alpina
Alpine woodsia
  Woodsia alpina
Bedstraw broomrape
  Orobanche caryophyllacea
Blue heath
  Phyllodoce caerulea
Brown galingale
  Cyperus fuscus
Cheddar pink
  Dianthus gratianopolitanus
Childling pink
  Petrorhagia nanteuilii
Diapensia
  Diapensia lapponica
Dickie's bladder-fern
  Cystopteris dickieana
Downy woundwort
  Stachys germanica
Drooping saxifrage
  Saxifraga cernua
Early spider-orchid
  Ophrys sphegodes
Fen Orchid
  Liparis loeselii
Fen violet
  Viola persicifolia
Field cow-wheat
  Melampyrum arvense
Field eryngo
  Eryngium campestre
Field wormwood
  Artemisia campestris
Ghost orchid
  Epipogium aphyllum
Greater yellow-rattle
  Rhinanthus serotinus

Jersey cudweed
  Gnaphalium luteoalbum
Killarney fern
  Trichomanes speciosum
Lady's-slipper
  Cypripedium calceolus
Late spider-orchid
  Ophrys fuciflora
Least lettuce
  Lactuca saligna
Limestone woundwort
  Stachys alpina
Lizard orchid
  Himantoglossum hircinum
Military orchid
  Orchis militaris
Monkey orchid
  Orchis simia
Norwegian sandwort
  Arenaria norvegica
Oblong woodsia
  Woodsia ilvensis
Oxtongue broomrape
  Orobanche loricata
Perennial knawel
  Scleranthus perennis
Plymouth pear
  Pyrus cordata
Purple spurge
  Euphorbia peplis
Red helleborine
  Cephalanthera rubra
Ribbon-leaved water-plantain
  Alisma gramineum
Rock cinquefoil
  Potentilla rupestris
Rock sea-lavender (two rare species)
  Limonium paradoxum/Limonium recurvum
Rough marsh-mallow
  Althaea hirsuta
Round-headed leek
  Allium sphaerocephalon
Sea knotgrass
  Polygonum maritimum
Sickle-leaved hare's-ear
  Bupleurum falcatum
Small Alison
  Alyssum alyssoides
Small hare's-ear
  Bupleurum baldense
Snowdon lily
  Lloydia serotina
Spiked speedwell
  Veronica spicata
Spring gentian
  Gentiana verna
Starfruit
  Damasonium alisma
Starved wood-sedge
  Carex depauperata
Teesdale sandwort
  Minuartia stricta

Thistle broomrape
  Orobanche reticulata
Triangular club-rush
  Scirpus triquetrus
Tufted saxifrage
  Saxifraga cespitosa
Water germander
  Teucrium scordium
Whorled solomon's-seal
  Polygonatum verticillatum
Wild cotoneaster
  Cotoneaster integerrimus
Wild gladiolus
  Gladiolus illyricus
Wood calamint
  Calamintha sylvatica

The following American plants are deemed to be endangered or threatened with extinction. Also listed are those plants that are treated as endangered or threatened because they are similar in appearance to those plants that are genuinely endangered or threatened. Again, do not pick or uproot them or collect their seed. If in doubt about a particular plant, contact the Department of Interior, U.S. Fish and Wildlife Service, Washington, D.C., 20240.

Antioch Dunes evening-primrose
  Oenothera deltoides ssp. *howellii*
Arizona agave
  Agave arizonica
Arizona cliffrose
  Cowania subintegra
Arizona hedgehog cactus
  Echinocereus triglochidiatus var. *arizonicus* (= *E. arizonicus*)
Ashy dogweed
  Dyssodia tephroleuca
Black lace cactus
  Echinocereus reichenbachii var. *albertii* (= *E. melanocentrus*)
Bunched arrowhead
  Sagittaria fasciculata
Bunched cory cactus
  Coryphantha ramillosa
Brady pincushion cactus
  Pediocactus bradyi (= *Toumeya b.*)
Carter's panicgrass
  Panicum carteri
Chapman rhododendron
  Rhododendron chapmanii
Clay-loving wild-buckwheat
  Eriogonum pelinophilum

Clay phacelia
  Phacelia argillacea
Contra Coasta wallflower
  Erysimum capitatum var. *angustatum*
Cooke's kokio
  Kokia cookei
Cuneate bidens
  Bidens cuneata
Davis' green pitaya
  Echinocereus viridiflorus var. *davisii* (= *E. davisii*)
Diamond Head schiedea
  Schiedea adamantis
Dwarf bear-poppy
  Arctomecon humilis
Eureka Dune grass
  Swallenia alexandrae
Eureka Valley evening-primrose
  Oenothera avita ssp. *eurekensis*
Ewa Plains 'akoko
  Euphorbia skottsbergii var. *kalaeloana*
Florida torreya
  Torreya taxifolia
Furbish lousewort
  Pedicularis furbishiae
Green pitcher plant
  Sarracenia oreophila
Gypsum wild-buckwheat
  Eriogonum gypsophilum
Hairy rattleweed
  Baptisia arachnifera
Haplostachys
  haplostachya var. *angustifolia*
Harper's beauty
  Harperocallis flava
Hawaiian vetch
  Vicia menziesii
Key tree-cactus
  Cereus robinii
Knowlton cactus
  Pediocactus knowltonii (= *P. bradyi* var. *k*, *Toumeya k.*)
Kuenzler hedgehog cactus
  Echinocereus fendleri var. *kuenzleri* (= *E. kuenzleri*, *E. hempelii* of authors, not Fobe)
Lee pincushion cactus
  Coryphantha sneedii var. *leei* (= *Escobaria l.*, *Mammillaria l.*)
  Lipochaeta veriosa
Lloyd's hedgehog cactus
  Echinocereus lloydii (= *E. roetteri* var. *l.*)
Lloyd's Mariposa cactus
  Neolloydia mariposensis (= *Echinocactus m.*, *Echinomastus m.*)
McDonald's rock-cress
  Arabis mcdonaldiana
MacFarlane's four-o'clock
  Mirabilis macfarlanei

McKittrick pennyroyal
Hedeoma apiculatum
Malheur wire-lettuce
Stephanomeria malheurensis
Mesa Verde cactus
Sclerocactus mesae-verdae
(= Coloradoa m., Echinocactus m.,
Pediocactus m.)
Mountain golden heather
Hudsonia montana
Navasota Ladies'-tresses
Spiranthes parksii
Nellie cory cactus
Coryphantha minima
(= C. nellieae, Escobaria n.,
Mammillaria n.)
Nichol's Turk's head cactus
· *Echinocactus horizonthalonius*
var. *nicholii*
Northern wild monkshood
Aconitum noveboracense
North Park phacelia
Phacelia formosula
Peebles Navajo cactus
Pediocactus peeblesianus var.
peeblesianus (= Echinocactus p.,
Navajoa p., Toumeya p., Utahia p.)
Persistent trillium
Trillium persistens
Presidio (= Raven's) manzanita
Arctostaphylos pungens var.
ravenii (= A. hookeri ssp. *ravenii)*
Purple-spined hedgehog cactus
Echinocereus engelmannii
var. *purpureus*
Robbins' cinquefoil
Potentilla robbinsiana
Rydberg milk-vetch
Astragalus perianus
Salt marsh bird's-beak
Cordylanthus maritimus
ssp. *maritimus*
San Clemente Island broom
Lotus dendroideus ssp. *traskiae*
(= L. scoparius ssp. *t.)*
San Clemente Island bush-mallow
Malacothamnus clementinus
San Clemente Island Indian
paintbrush
Castilleja grisea

San Clemente Island larkspur
Delphinium kinkiense
San Diego mesa mint
Pogogyne abramsii
San Francisco Peaks groundsel
Senecio franciscanus
Santa Barbara Island liveforever
Dudleya traskiae
Siler pincushion cactus
Pediocactus sileri (= Echinocactus
s., Utahia s.)
Small whorled pogonia
Isotria medeoloides
Sneed pincushion cactus
Coryphantha sneedii var. *sneedii*
(= Escobaria s., Mammillaria s.)
Solano grass
Tuctoria mucronata
(= Orcuttia m.)
Spineless hedgehog cactus
Echinocereus triglochidiatus var.
inermis (= E. coccineus var. *i.,*
E. phoeniceus var. *i.)*
Stenogyne
angustifolia var. *angustifolia*
Tennessee purple coneflower
Echinacea tennesseensis
Texas poppy-mallow
Callirhoe scabriuscula
Texas wild-rice
Zizania texana
Tobusch fishook cactus
Ancistrocactus tobuschii
(= Echinocactus t., Mammillaria t.)
Todsen's pennyroyal
Hedeoma todsenii
Truckee barberry
Mahonia sonnei (= Berberis s.)
Uinta Basin hookless cactus
Sclerocactus glaucus
(= Echinocactus g., E. subglaucus,
E. whipplei var. *g., Pediocactus g.,*
S. franklinii, S. whipplei var. *g.)*
Virginia round-leaf birch
Betula uber
Wright fishook cactus
Sclerocactus wrightiae
(= Pediocactus w.)

ACKNOWLEDGEMENTS

The author and publishers thank the following photographers and organizations for their kind permission to reproduce the photographs on the following pages:
Page 10 below right, the estate of Cicely M. Barker/Blackie & Son Ltd.; page 13, Bridgeman Art Library; page 10 left, Mary Evans Picture Library; page 11, Scala/Firenze; pages 132 above left, 134 centre, 137 centre right, 138 below left, 139 centre right, and below right, Harry Smith Horticultural Photographic Collection; page 12, Stadelsches, Kunstinstitut, Frankfurt.

Special photography:
Pages 127 centre, 128 below, 130 below, 131 centre above and right, 132 below left, 134 above, 135 below left, 136 below left, 138 above left, Michael Boys; pages 127 above and below, 130 above and centre, 131 above left, 133 above right, centre and below, 134 below, 136 above right, 137 above and below right, 138 centre left, 138 above, 140 above left, Jerry Harpur; page 129 above, John Sims; pages 128 above, 129 centre and below, 132 centre left and above right, 133 above left, 135 below centre and centre right, 137 above and centre left, 138 above right, 140 centre and below left, George Wright.

All other photographs by Philip Dowell.

The author and publishers are extremely grateful to all those who kindly loaned the accessories which appear in the photographs on the following pages:
Page 66 *Boston fern*, 68 *bay trees and containers*, 80 *cachepot*, Clifton Nurseries; page 29 *glasses*, 49 *fruit bowl*, 63 *table*, 77 *trolley*, 104 *glass candlesticks*, 122 *mirror*, The Conran Shop; page 33 *vase*, 70 *plate*, 82 *cake tin*, 124 *basket*, David Mellor, Covent Garden; page 17 *fireback*, Gas Log Fire Emporium, George Street, London W1; page 25 *crockery and cutlery*, 27 *flan dishes*, 36 *vases*, 39 *cutlery and casserole dish*, 99 *umbrella stand and umbrella* The General Trading Company, 144 Sloane Street, London SW1; page 15 *table*, 21 *table*, 25 *paper blind*, 96 *table*, 103 and 104 *paper blind* Habitat (branches throughout Britain); page 25 *clay pots*, 30 *cutlery*, 52 *mug*, 64 *ash trays*, 77 *vases*, 81 *cachepot*, 86 *glass dishes*, 96 *glasses*, 99 *carpet* Heal's, 196 Tottenham Court Road, London W1; page 71 *basket*, Ken Turner Flowers, 8 Avery Row, London W1; page 33 *painting by Richard Lynn*, by courtesy of Richard Salmon.

Acanthus 80, 97, *114*, 116
Acer saccharinum see Maple, sugar
Adhesives 120
Aftercare 111-12
Agapanthus 26, 34; 'Headbourne Hybrids' *136*
Alchemilla mollis see Lady's mantle
Alder 34, 72, 76
Allium see Ornamental onion
Almond, flowering 70, *70*, 71
Alstroemeria see Lily, Peruvian
Alum 80–82
Alyssum 24, 43, 127, 133
Amaranthus caudatus 'Viridis' see Love-lies-bleeding
Amaryllis 23, 26, 110
Anemone 30, 42, 96, 117, 132; *A. coronaria* 'De Caen' 45, *96*, *132*; Japanese 60; wood 15
Apple 42, 43; blossom 72
Arctotis grandis/hybrida see Daisy, African
Artemisia 58; *A. absinthum* 'Lambrook Silver' 58; *A. arborescens* 58
Artichokes, globe 42, 50, *51*, 80
Artificial flowers 59, 76–8, *77*
Asparagus 47, 120; *A. medeoloides* 47; *A. plumosus* 47
Aspidistra 83
Aster novi-belgii see Daisy, Michaelmas
Athyrium filix-femina see Fern, lady
Aubrieta 24, 98
Autumnal decorations 35–6
Azalea 59, 66; 'Hino-crimson' 60; Kurume 60; 'Stewartsonian' 60

Baby's breath see Gypsophila
Bachelor's buttons see Cornflowers
Balm, lemon 48, 86
Bark, ornamental 75–6
Basil, sweet 48, 86, 88
Bay 38, 48, *68*, 69, 86
Beech 59, 60, 72, 83, 84, 116; purple 57
Begonia 70; *B. boweri* 70; *B. rex* 70
Bellis perennis see Daisy, European
Bells of Ireland 80, 82, 87
Berberis 55, 116
Bergenia 34; *B. cordifolia* 60, 83, 84
Berries 35, 38, 39, 47, 60, 61, *64–5*, 68, 74–5. 79, 86, 110
Bird of paradise 125
Blackberry 16, 74, *64–5*
Bluebell 16, 116, 133
Borax 80, 82
Box 83
Brachycome iberidifolia see Daisy, Swan River
Bracken *64–5*, 83
Branches/twigs 20, 24, 34, 39, 53, *70*, *71*, 76; cutting 108. shaping 76
Bulbs 73, *73*, 110, 117, *134*, *135*

Bulrush 78, 80, 87
Buttercup 10, *14*, 16
Butterfly flower see Schizanthus
Buying flowers 105–7

Calluna vulgaris 'Blazeaway'/'Gold Haze' see Heathers, golden
Camellia 26, 83, 109, 110, 112, 131; *C. japonica* 'Alba Simplex' 131; *C. j.* 'Mathotiana Alba' 131; *C.* × *williamsii* 'Donation' 131
Cardiocrinum giganteum see Lily, giant
Carnation 11, 12, 19, 20, *21*, *33*, 38, 44, *68*, 82, 95, 106, 122, 134–5; cutting 108
Catkins 72, 73, 83
Cedar, blue 58; Japanese 60
Cedrus atlantica 'Glauca' see Cedar, blue
Centaurea cyanus see Cornflowers
Chamomile 88
Cherry fruit *49*; blossom 72
Chestnut 47, 72, 98; sweet *55*, *64–5*, 75, 84
Chicken wire 38–9, 79, 117–18
Chincherinchee *68*, *96*, 116, 135
Chinese lantern 80
Choisya ternata see Mexican orange
Christmas decorations 38–9, 68
Chrysanthemums 16, 20, 26, 35, 38, 44, 45, *51*, 56, 60, 65, *68*, 69, 74, 75, 83, 97, 101, *102*, *103*, 107, 110, 116, 122, *123*; *C. carinatum* 139; *C. coronarium* 139; *C. corymbosum* 88; 'Hunstanton' *137*; *C. maximum* 139, *139*; tricolour 139; *C. uliginosum* 139; 'White Spider' *137*
Cineraria 32, 66
Citrus fruit 42, *46*, 88; blossom 10, 66
Clematis 26, *51*, 82, 83, *104–5*, 110–11, 113, 132. 'Ville de Lyon' *132*
Clover 16, 86
Coleus 56, 139
Conditioning 108–11
Conifers 38
Containers 93–103
Convallaria majalis see Lily-of-the-valley
Coral bells 42, 126
Cornflowers *19*, 106, 135, *135*
Cornus see Dogwood
Corylus avellana 'Contorta' see Hazel, corkscrew
Cotinus 55, *114*; *C. coggygria* 'Royal Purple' 57, 140
Cotoneaster 75, 83
Cow parsley 15, *17*, 23, 26, 32, 80, 97, 135
Crab apple 72, 74, 98, *114*
Crocus 69, *73*, 135; *C. tomasinianus* 135
Cryptomeria japonica see Cedar, Japanese

Currant, flowering 70, 72
Cut Flower Nutrient 108, 112–13
Cyclamen 66
Cypripedium see Orchid, lady's slipper

Daffodils 73, 77, 82, 106, 110, 128, 134, *134*; miniature 24
Dahlia *8*, 20, 26, 43, 45, 56, 60, 82, 109, 116, 122, 138–9; 'Kay Helen' *139*
Daisy 9, 10, *14*, 16, 24, 38, 42, 43, 45, *49*, 96, 101, 122, 139–40; African *139*, 139–40; barberton *114*, 139, *139*; European 140, *140*; glorious 140; kingfisher 140; Michaelmas 75, 110, 140; moon 139; Shasta 107, 139, *139*; Swan River 140
Dandelion 75, 97, 109
Daphne laureola 9
Delphinium *22*, 23, 32, 80, 82, 98, 107, 109, 132, *132*
Dianthus barbatus see Sweet William
Dianthus chinensis see Pinks
Dogwood 54, 75
Dryopteris filix-mas see Fern, male

Echinops see Thistle, globe
Elder 56–7, *64–5*, 74
Elaeagnus 83, 84, 116
Endymion non-scriptus see Bluebell
Eremurus robustus see Lily, foxtail
Erica carnea 'Aurea' see Heather, golden
Erica cinerea 'Golden Drop' see Heather, golden
Eryngium see Holly, sea
Essential oils 86, 88, 89
Eucalyptus *55*, 58, 107
Euphorbia 62, 109; *E. characias* 62; *E. lathyris* 62; *E. myrsinites* 20, 62; *E. robbiae* 62; *E. wolfenii* 62

Fagus sylvatica 'Purpurea'/'Riversii' see Beech, purple
Fatsia japonica 34, 84
Feathers 87–8
Felicia bergeriana see Daisy, kingfisher
Fennel 48, 50
Fern 32, 62, *63*, 78, 83, 86; asparagus 47, 51, 134; Boston *67*, 70; hart's tongue 62; lady 62; maidenhair 70; male 62
Ficus benjamina see Fig, weeping
Fig 42; weeping 69
Fireplaces *17*, *19*, 32
Floral ball, 19–20, *81*, 121–3, *123*
Flowerheads 23, 26, 28–30, 101, 137
Florists' vials 38, 69, 119
Forcing 70, 72, 73
Forget-me-not 24, 43, 117, 132, 138, *138*
Foxglove 10, 14, 15

Fruit and vegetables 41–51, *43*, *44*, *51*, 66, 70, 74, 86, 119
Fuchsias 54; *F. magellanica* 'Versicolor' 54

Galax *34*, 107
Gentian *28*, 97
Geranium 12, 32, 42, 78, *100*, 126; regal 69; scented 69, 88; zonal 69
Gerbera jamesonii see Daisy, barberton
Gladioli 48, 106, 107, 111, 116, 125
Gloriosa see Lily, glory
Glycerine 83–4
Grapevine, ornamental 57
Grasses, dried 79, *81*; pampas 80
Gypsophila paniculata 43, *68*, 86, *114*, 133, 134; 'Flamingo' 133; 'Pink Star' 133; 'Rosy Veil' 133, *133*

Hazel, corkscrew 34, 76; witch 70
Heather 80, 84, 101, 110; golden 57, 60
Hedera colchica 'Dentata Variegata'/ 'Paddy's Pride' see Ivy, Persian
Hedera helix see Ivy
Helianthus annuus 'Sunburst' see Sunflower
Heliotrope 86, 88, 109
Helleborus niger see Rose, Christmas
Hemerocallis see Lily, day
Herbs 48, 50; in pot-pourri 88, 89
Hermodactylus tuberosus see Iris, snake's head
Heuchera cylindrica 'Chartreuse'/ 'Greenfinch' see Coral bells
Holly 38, 39, 43, 54, 75; sea 80, 101, *102*, *103*, 116
Hollyhock 80, 98, *99*
Honeysuckle 16, 78
Hornbeam 60, 72, 81
Hosta *52–3*, 54, 61, 80; *H. sieboldiana* 61; *H. undulata* 61
Hyacinth 9, 66, 69, 73, 110, 133; grape 24, 133, *133*
Hydrangea 78, 80, 84, 109

Iris, *12*, 28, *95*, 106, 120, 137; Algerian 137; *I. florentina* 88; miniature 24, 60, *73*; *I. pallida* 137; *I. reticulata* 137; snake's head 137; *I. stylosa* 137; *I. unguicularis* 137; *I. xiphium* 137
Ivy 20, 23, 35, 38, 42, 43, *46*, 50, *52–3*, 54, 60–1, *64–5*, 74, 76, 78, 84, 98; *Hedera helix* 'Buttercup' 61; *H. h* 'Cristata' 61; elephant's-ear 61; *H. h* 'Glacia' 45; 'Gold Heart' 44, *52–3*; Persian 61; *H. h* 'Sagittifolia' 61

Jasmine 88, summer 138, *138*; winter 73
Jasminum nudiflorum see Jasmine, winter

Jasminum officinale see Jasmine, summer

Lady's mantle 42, 54, 126
Landscapes, miniature 23–4
Larch *55, 59*, 138
Lathyrus odoratus 130
Laurel, Portuguese 83, *95*, 116
Lavender 80, *85*, 86, *87*, 88, 89
Leaf vase *95*
Lilac 38, 73, 88, 109, 129, 130–1; *Syringa vulgaris* 'Firmament' *131*
Lily 12, 23, 34, *36*, 38, 106, 126, 135–7; African 136, *136*; arum 106, 136, *136*; day 136; foxtail 23, 116, 136, *136*; giant 23, 136; glory 136; Guernsey 136; madonna *12*, 136, *136*; Peruvian 101, 116, 136–7, *137*; plantain 61; regal 135; sword 125; tiger *10*, 136; water 26, 113
Lily-of-the-valley 16, 24, 69, 88, 128, *128*, 133
Lilium candidum see Lily, madonna
Lilium regale see Lily, regal
Lilim tigrinum see Lily, tiger
Love-lies-bleeding 20, 80
Lupin 109, 116

Magnolia 34, 83; evergreen 54, 56, *59*; *M. grandiflora* 'Exmouth' 56
Mahonia japonica 58, 74, 83, 84
Malus 'Golden Hornet'/'John Downie' see Crab apple
Maple 58; Japanese 72; sugar 58
Marigold 75, 82, 88, 97; French *29*, 45; pot 44; in pot-pourri *87*
Maypole 20
Meconopsis betonicifolia see Poppy, Himalayan blue
Meconopsis cambrica see Poppy, Welsh
Mexican orange *77*, 83
Mignonette 86, 88
Mimosa 84, 111, 116
Mint 48, 50, 88
Mirrors 32, 121, *123*
Misting 24, 72, 94, 112, *113*, 117, 119
Mistletoe 38, 39, 43
Mock orange see Philadelphus
Moss 19, 23–4, 38, 47, *64–5*, 66, *74*, 76, 93, 94, 120–1; artificial 121
Muscari latifolium see Hyacinth, grape
Myosotis alpestris see Forget-me-not
Myrtle 88

Narcissus 73, 110; 'Paper White' 134; see also Daffodils
Nasturtium 44, 47, 101, 133, *133*; 'Tom Thumb' 133
National holidays 38, *39*
Nerine bowdenii 136; *N. sarniensis* 136
Onopordum acanthium see Thistle, giant

Orchid 38, 103, 119, 122, 129; cymbidium 129; lady's slipper 129, *129*; moth 32, 129. odontoglossum 129; vanda 129
Ornamental onion 51, 80, 110
Ornithogalum umbellatum see Chincherinchee
Orris root 88

Paeony 26, *29*, 97, 106, 116, 129–30; 'Beersheba' 130; *Paeonia delavayi* 129; 'Edulis Supreme' 130; *P. lactiflora* 'Karl Rosenfeld' *129*; *P. lutea* 129; *P. officinalis* 'Rosea-plena' *129*; *P. suffruticosa* 129; tree 129; 'White Wings' 130; 'Wrinkled White' 130
Pansy 25, *27*, 75, 82, 127, 128, 132, *132, 133*, 'Bowles Black' 132; 'Floral Dance Mixed' 132
Papaver orientale see Poppy, oriental
Papaver somniferum see Poppy, opium
Paphiopedilum 129, *129*
Parsley 48, *51*
Passion flower 26, 116
Pear 42; blossom 72
Peat 66, 71
Periwinkle, rosy *10*; variegated 54
Philadelphus 36, 109, 126; *P. coronarius* 'Aureus' 56
Phalaenopsis see Orchid, moth
Phlox 42
Phormium see Flax, New Zealand
Phyllitis scolopendrium see Fern, hart's-tongue
Picking flowers 107–8
'Pig squeak' see *Bergenia*
'Pincushion flower' see Scabious
Pinholders 118
Pinks 11, 48, 58, 69, 82, 88, 101, 106, 108, 122, 126, *134*, 134–5
Plastic foam 20, 24, 38–9, 79, 98, 101, 117
Plasticine 39, 118, 119
Plum/prune 42, *70*; blossom 57, 72
Poinsettia 38, 62
Polyanthus 24
Polygonatum see Solomon's seal
Poppy 16, 80, 82, 109, 130; California tree 130; fried egg 130; Himalayan blue 130, *130*; Matlija 130; opium 130; oriental 130, *130*; Welsh 130
Polystyrene 117
Poor man's orchid see Schizanthus
Poplar, Gilead 56; white 56
Populus alba 'Richardii' see Poplar, white
Populus candicans 'Aurora' see Poplar, white
Pot-et-fleur 67, 69–70
Pot-pourri 86–91, *87*
Preserving 78–84
Primrose 12, 15, 24, 69, 133

Privet 54, 74
Protea 80, 84
Prunus cerasifera 'Pissardii' see Plum, blossom
Pyrethrum 107, 122

Queen Anne's lace 15, *17*, 23, 26, 32, 80, 97, 135
Quince, flowering 70, 72; fruit 86

Raphiolepis umbellata 63
Reviving flowers 115–16
Rhododendron 42, *55*, 56, *64–5*, 84, 109, 112, 114, 138, *138*; *R. grande* 56
Rhubarb flowers 23, 50, 97
Rhus typhina see Staghorn sumach
Romneya coulteri see Poppy, California tree
Rosemary 48, 86, 88, 89
Rose 10, 12, 16, 20, 23, 24, 41, 43, *43*, 48, 50, 54, 57, 58, 61, 65, 73, 74, 75, 79, 82, *82*, 83, 86, 96, 98, 103, 106, 111, *120*, 122, 126–7, 130; Alba 126; 'Blue Moon' 131; Bourbon 126; buds 30, *37*, 38, *44*, 48, 70; Christmas 39; damask 88, 126; *Rosa damascena* 'Versicolor' 10; 'Elizabeth of Glamis' 132; 'Fleur Cowles' 11; floribunda 126; *R. gallica* 126, *126*; hips 24, 47, 57–8, *64–5*, 83; hybrid tea 11; 'Iceberg' *126*, 127; 'Madame Hardy' *126*; miniature 69; moss 10, 16, 88, 127; 'Old Velvet Moss' 127; petals *37*, 88; rugosa 88; 'William Lobb' 127; Yellow Rose of Texas 10; York and Lancaster 10
Rudbeckia hirta 45, 107, 140; 'Marmalade' *140*
Rue 57–8, *63*
Ruta graveolens 'Jackman's Blue' see Rue

Sage 48; variegated 54
Salvia officinalis 'Icterina'/'Tricolor' see Sage
Sambucus nigra 'Aurea' see Elder
Sambucus racemosa 'Plumosa Aurea' see Elder
Sand 80, 82, *92–3*, 120
Santolina chamaecyparissus 88
Scabious 34, *35*, 106, 134; *Scabiosa atropurpurea* 134, *134*; *S. caucasica* 134
Schizanthus 138; 'Monarch Strain' *138*
Seedheads/pods 60, 79, 80, 83, *114*
Senecio 55, 63, 114
Silica gel 80–2
Silk flowers *59*, 76, 77, *77*, 78
Smilax 47
Smoke tree 57, 140
Snowdrop 16, 24, 38, 60, 69, *73*
Solomon's seal 83

Sorbus *64–5*, 75; *S. hupehensis* 75; 'Joseph Rock' 75
Spices for pot-pourri 88
Spurge 62, 109; caper 62
Staghorn sumach 60
Star of Bethlehem see Chincherinchee
Statice 78, 80, 116
Stock 75, 106; Brompton *51*; night-scented 88
Strelitzia reginae see Bird of paradise
Sunflower 23, 26, 101, 140, *140*; 'Autumn Beauty' 140; 'Russian Giant' 140
Sweet peas 11, 30, 43, 88, 122, 130, *130*; 'Jet Set' 130; 'Little Sweetheart' 130
Summer decorations 34–5, 42
Sweet William 30, 43, 135, *135*
Sycamore 72, 75, 98
Syringa vulgaris see Lilac

Tablecloths 34–5, *120*
Thistle *52–3*, 80; giant 61; globe 116; wild 16
Thyme 88, 89
Tools/equipment 105, 116–23
Tropaeolum majus see Nasturtium
Tulip 34, 47, 50, 73, 77, 78, 82, *92–3*, 94, 106, 111, 120, 127, *127*, 133; 'Black Parrot' 127; 'Fantasy' 127; miniature 'Viridiflora' 127

Valeriana officinalis 88
Verbena, lemon 88; in pot pourri *87*
Viburnum *64–5*, 73, 86; *fragrans (farreri)* 60; winter 60
Viola blanda/odorata see Violet
Viola gracilis see Pansy
Viola labradorica 'Purpurea' see Violet, purple-leaved
Viola x wittrockiana see Pansy
Violet 9, 15, 69, 88, 97, 111, *111*, 117, 128; 'Coeur d'Alsace' 128; 'Duchesse du Parme' 128; in pot-pourri *87*; 'Princess of Wales' 128; purple-leaved 128, *128*
Virgin's Bower see Clematis
Vine, ornamental 57, 86
Vitis coignetiae see Vine, ornamental
Vitis vinifera 'Brandt'/'Purpurea' see Vine, ornamental

Wallflower 24, 75
Whitebeam 72, 75
Wild flowers 14–16, 96
Willow 76, 83; pussy 72
Windows 31–2, 89

Yarrow 84; dried 78, 80

Zantedeschia aethiopica see Lily, arum
Zinnia 24, 30, 42, 45, 82, 126; 'Envy' 42

●●